cooking with
RICE

cooking with
RICE

Laurence and Gilles Laurendon

photographs by Akiko Ida
design John Bentham

HACHETTE
Illustrated

ABOUT RICE

THERE ARE AROUND 8,000 VARIETIES OF RICE WORLDWIDE. Some are characterized by their flavour, colour and/or the shape of their grains, others by their method of cultivation or the type of processing received after harvesting.

The varieties of rice used for the recipes in this book are readily available in stores and super-markets. Today, you can buy good-quality precooked rice (ideal for microwaving) and quick-cook rice, as well as frozen precooked rice.

A wide range of products is made with rice, including rice noodles, rice biscuits made from puffed rice, and the thin rice pancakes used to make spring rolls. And not forgetting the crea-med rice popular in Middle-Eastern cuisine and the amazing rice cakes (*mochi*) made in Japan using sticky rice – you'll find recipes for these in the following pages.

Steamed (or pretreated) long-grain rice

The rice is cleaned and soaked in hot water, then steamed, and dried. It has virtually no starch and is quick and easy to prepare. It doesn't stick and retains most of its vitamins.

Basmati rice

A perfumed rice from India and Pakistan. Its long, narrow grains are ideally suited to Indian and Oriental cuisine.

Jasmine rice

A white rice from Vietnam and Thailand with a delicate jasmine fragrance. The long, fine grains make excellent steamed rice.

Japanese rice

A short-grain rice with round grains that is ideal for making sushi.

Semi-brown rice

The part-milled, beige-coloured grains retain a high proportion of their vitamins and don't take as long to cook as brown rice. In short, a rice that has no disadvantages.

Brown (wholegrain) rice

A beige-coloured rice that is very rich in vitamins and mineral salts because only the outer husk is removed. The only disadvantage is that it takes at least 45 minutes to cook.

CREOLE RICE

Plenty of water

This is the most widely used method of cooking rice in the world. It is also the simplest and can be used for most varieties of rice.

There are two ways of cooking rice in water. You can either add the rice to a large pan of boiling water and leave it to cook, uncovered, like pasta (in which case the rice should "float freely" in the water), or you can add 1 part rice to 1½ parts warm water or stock, cover, and leave to cook until all the liquid has been absorbed.

Stocks and flavourings

Depending on the recipe, you can use stock (chicken, vegetable or beef) or flavour the cooking water with spices (cinnamon, chilli powder, ginger, nutmeg, cloves), orange or lemon rind, or aromatic herbs (thyme, bay, rosemary, chives, parsley, coriander, lemongrass).

Basic recipe

Serves 4
Preparation: 5 minutes
Cooking: 12–15 minutes

Rinse the rice under cold running water until the water runs through clear, then drain in a sieve or strainer. Bring 300 ml/ ½ pint water or stock to the boil in a large pan. Season with salt and pepper, add 175 g/6 oz/ generous ¾ cup rice and cover with a tight-fitting lid. Bring the water back to the boil, reduce the heat and leave to simmer gently, without removing the lid, for 12–15 minutes. The rice should still have a bit of bite (al dente). Drain and serve immediately or keep warm.

STEAMED RICE

Varieties of rice

Steaming produces rice that is light and fluffy, and extremely tender. It is an ideal way of cooking "sticky rice", but you can also use it for all varieties of long- and short-grain rice, provided you soak the grains in water for at least 1 hour beforehand. The longer the rice is soaked, the quicker it will cook. You can also use a rice cooker, which steams the rice and keeps it warm.

Rice cooker

An electric rice cooker produces perfectly cooked rice with well-separated grains.

Perfumed rice

You can either flavour the cooking water or place aromatic herbs in the perforated container or basket of a steamer – choose from marjoram, mint, thyme, lime leaves, lemongrass, rosemary, lemon or orange rind.

Basic recipe

Serves 4
Preparation: 5 minutes
Soaking: at least 1 hour
Cooking: 25 minutes

Pour the rice into a large bowl, cover with water and leave to soak for at least 1 hour, or overnight if possible. Drain well and place in the perforated container or basket of a steamer, preferably lined with a piece of muslin or cheesecloth. Bring the water in the steamer (or pan of water) to the boil and place the container or basket above the boiling water. Cover with a tight-fitting lid and leave to cook for about 25 minutes. If you have lined the steamer basket with muslin, remove the lid and leave the rice to stand for a minute when it is cooked.

PILAU RICE

Method

This method involves frying the rice lightly in hot fat (butter or oil) before cooking in a covered pan in hot water or stock: allow about 1½ parts liquid to 1 part rice. You can cook most varieties of rice using this method, but it is particularly well suited to long-grain rice.

Spicy pilau rice

Add 1 teaspoon ground turmeric and 1 teaspoon ground ginger to the cooking stock: a simple idea that adds flavour to the rice – and aroma to the kitchen.

Quick recipe idea

Heat a lightly oiled frying pan, add 2 good pinches curry powder and 1 onion (peeled and chopped) and mix well. Then add 300 g/10 oz diced boned skinless chicken breasts and cook for 4–5 minutes, stirring continuously. Serve with pilau rice.

Butter and/or olive oil

To fry the rice, you can use a knob of butter or a little olive oil, or a combination of the two. The butter adds richness, while the oil can be heated to a higher temperature. This is ideal if you want rice with a firm but creamy texture.

Basic recipe

Serves 4
Preparation: 5 minutes
Cooking: 12–15 minutes

175 g/6 oz/generous ¾ cup rice
300 ml/½ pint water or stock

Heat 1 tablespoon oil in a high-sided cooking pot or flameproof casserole and add the rice. Stir with a wooden spoon to ensure all the grains are well coated with oil. Add the hot water or stock, season with salt and pepper, bring to the boil and cover with a tight-fitting lid. Reduce the heat and simmer gently for 12–15 minutes.

RISOTTO

Cooking by absorption

This method of cooking rice is mainly used for preparing risottos. Start by lightly frying the rice in hot fat (usually olive oil), then add the hot water or stock, a ladle at a time, until it has all been completely absorbed. It is a method that requires just a little bit more attention as each ladleful must be fully absorbed before adding the next.

Listening to the rice

A good risotto is cooked "by ear" – listen carefully and start adding the stock when the rice begins to "sing". A risotto should simmer very gently and never bubble or boil. When the rice is cooked, add grated Parmesan cheese to give a deliciously creamy texture.

Arborio and Carnaroli

Choosing the right rice is crucial – the best risottos are made with Arborio Superfino or Carnaroli and, if available, Vialone Nano.

Stock ideas

Depending on the recipe, you can use vegetable or chicken stock. For those extra special occasions, choose an aromatic fish or game stock, or perhaps a veal stock base.

"Mantecare" (*thicken*)

When the rice is cooked, add knobs of butter and Parmesan cheese, and leave to stand for 1–2 minutes. Then mix briskly with a wooden spoon to give the rice a thick, creamy texture The art of making a good risotto lies in this simple but effective technique.

Basic recipe

Serves 4
Preparation: 5 minutes
Cooking: 25 minutes

1 litre/1¾ pints/4 cups stock
2 tablespoons oil
200 g/7 oz/1 cup risotto rice
1½ tablespoons butter
50 g/1¾ oz/½ cup freshly grated Parmesan cheese

Heat the stock gently in a pan, and, in another, heavy-bottomed pan, heat the oil. Add the rice to the oil, fry lightly for a few minutes and then mix with a wooden spoon so that the grains are well coated with oil. Add a ladle of warm stock to the rice pan, stir until it has been completely absorbed and then add another ladle. Continue to add the rest of the stock in this way, waiting for each ladleful to be absorbed before adding the next. Remove the rice from the heat, add knobs of butter and grated Parmesan cheese and leave to stand for 1–2 minutes. Mix briskly with a wooden spoon to give the rice a thick, creamy texture. Serve immediately.

How to use
chopsticks ...

EASY RICE

Rice with minty yogurt

In a bowl mix together 150 g/5 oz/$2/3$ cup thick, creamy yogurt with a few chopped mint leaves. Season lightly with salt and pepper.

Serve steamed or boiled rice in small bowls and top with the minty yogurt. Serve the rice warm.

Rice with chutney

Serve steamed or boiled rice in small bowls with a teaspoon of chutney. Serve the rice warm.

Rice with soy sauce

Serve steamed or boiled rice in small bowls and drizzle with a little dark soy sauce. Serve the rice hot.

Rice with Parmesan cheese shavings

Use a potato peeler to cut shavings from a piece of Parmesan cheese.

Scatter the shavings over the rice, season generously with black pepper and serve immediately.

Rice with Roquefort cheese sauce

Crumble 100 g/3½ oz Roquefort cheese into a pan and add 100 ml/3½ fl oz/scant ½ cup crème fraîche (or plain yogurt) and 2 tablespoons white wine. Melt over low heat for 5 minutes.

Pour into an electric blender and give a short burst (about 3 seconds). Season with black pepper and serve with steamed or boiled rice.

Orange rice

Add the rice to a pan containing 1 part boiling salted water and 1 part orange juice, cover and simmer gently for about 15 minutes. Leave to stand for 5 minutes, without removing the lid, before serving.

Sprinkle with a little finely grated orange rind and a pinch of soft brown sugar. Serve warm.

Coconut rice

Add the rice to a pan of boiling salted coconut milk flavoured with lemon rind, cover and simmer gently for about 15 minutes. Leave to stand for 5 minutes, without removing the lid, before serving.

Coconut rice makes an ideal accompaniment for Indian cuisine.

Curried rice

Add 1 teaspoon mild curry powder to a pan of salted water, bring to the boil and add the rice. Cover and leave to simmer gently for about 15 minutes. Leave to stand for 5 minutes, without removing the lid, before serving.

Spinach and mint rice

Serves 4
Preparation: 10 minutes
Cooking: 25 minutes

200 g/7 oz spinach
1 teaspoon cumin seeds
300 ml/¹/₂ pint/1¹/₄ cups vegetable or
chicken stock
175 g/6 oz/generous ³/₄ cup basmati rice,
washed and drained
1 teaspoon fresh ginger, grated
1 onion, peeled and chopped
2 teaspoons mint leaves, chopped
oil, for cooking
salt and freshly ground black pepper

Rinse, drain and dry the spinach (in a salad
spinner or a clean dish towel), then chop finely.
Heat 1 tablespoon oil in a high-sided cooking pot
or flameproof casserole, lightly fry the cumin
seeds and add the chopped spinach. Cook over
medium heat for about 10 minutes, stirring at
regular intervals.

While the spinach is cooking, heat the stock in a
separate pan.

Heat 1 tablespoon oil in a heavy-bottomed pan
and add the rice, mixing well so that the grains
are well coated with oil. Then pour the warm
stock onto the rice. Season with salt and pepper,
bring to the boil, cover and leave to cook over
low heat for about 15 minutes.

While the rice is cooking, heat 1 tablespoon oil in
a frying pan and lightly fry the ginger and onion
over moderately high heat, stirring continuously
so that they don't stick to the pan.

Add the rice to the pot or casserole containing
the spinach. Stir in the chopped mint, mix well
and leave to simmer for a few minutes. Taste and
season with salt and pepper if required.

Serve hot with the fried onion and ginger.

Risotto rice

The large, round grains have a high starch content and are ideal for making all kinds of risottos. In particular, Arborio and Carnaroli varieties produce a creamy, melting texture. Vialone Nano is another excellent risotto rice, but is less readily available.

Red Camargue rice

A whole rice from the French region of Camargue, full of flavour with an attractive reddish colour. A delicious rice that comes highly recommended.

Black rice

This whole rice, available from delicatessens and the foreign food sections of major supermarkets, is almost too beautiful to cook. It is prepared like risotto rice.

Wild rice

The grains look like little black sticks and have a deliciously nutty flavour. They are in fact the seeds of an aquatic grass (*zizania*) which is native to the northern United States. It is readily available in the UK.

Surinam rice

This rice from the small republic of Surinam, in the northeast of South America, has very long, fine grains. It goes well with sauces and makes an ideal accompaniment for slow-cooked and simmered dishes.

Sticky rice

A short- or medium-grain rice widely used in Asian cuisine. The high starch content of the grains means that they "stick" to each other, but should not be confused with badly cooked rice. Sticky rice is used in the preparation of sweet or savoury rice balls and rice cakes.

Swordfish with star anise

Serves 4
Preparation: 5 minutes
Cooking: 15 minutes

175 g/6 oz/generous ³/₄ cup long-grain rice
300 ml/¹/₂ pint/1¹/₄ cups hot water
2 star anise flowers
2 pinches mild chilli powder
4 swordfish steaks
oil, for cooking
salt and freshly ground black pepper

Rinse the rice several times in cold water until the water runs clear and then drain through a sieve or strainer. Turn into a heavy-bottomed pan and cover with the measured hot water. Season with salt and add the star anise and chilli powder. Bring to the boil, cover and cook over low heat for about 15 minutes.

Remove the pan from the heat and leave to stand for 5 minutes, without removing the lid.

Coat the swordfish steaks with a little oil and season with salt and pepper. Heat a lightly oiled frying pan over medium heat, and fry the steaks for 3–4 minutes on each side.

Remove the star anise from the rice pan, separate the grains with a fork and serve immediately with the fish steaks. You can use the star anise to garnish the rice.

Sole with grapefruit, ginger and honey sauce

Serves 4
Preparation: 5 minutes
Cooking: 15 minutes

juice of ¹/₂ grapefruit
1 teaspoon fresh ginger, grated
2 teaspoons clear honey
300 ml/¹/₂ pint/1¹/₄ cups water
125 g/4 oz/generous ¹/₂ cup long-grain rice, washed and drained
8 sole fillets
salt and freshly ground black pepper

Put the grapefruit juice, grated ginger and honey into a small pan. Bring to the boil, remove from the heat, cover and leave to infuse.

Place the measured water in a large pan, bring to the boil and season with salt. Add the rice and stir well. Cover, reduce the heat and leave to simmer gently for about 12 minutes – the rice should be tender but still retain a bit of bite (al dente). Just before serving, separate the grains with a fork.

Meanwhile, put some water in the base of a steamer and bring to the boil, place the sole fillets in the perforated container or basket, cover and leave to cook for about 8 minutes.

Whisk the grapefruit, ginger and honey sauce and drizzle over the sole fillets.

Season with salt and pepper and serve immediately with the rice.

Note: Ideally, the fish should be served hot and the sauce cold.

Rice with Gorgonzola cheese cream

Serves 4
Preparation: 5 minutes
Cooking: 20 minutes

125 g/4 oz/generous ¹/₂ cup long-grain rice, washed and drained
300 ml/¹/₂ pint/1¹/₄ cups hot water
1 onion, peeled and chopped
1 sprig fresh thyme, chopped
150 g/5 oz Gorgonzola cheese
400 ml/14 fl oz/1³/₄ cups milk
oil, for cooking
salt and freshly ground black pepper
2 tablespoons chopped flat-leaf parsley

Heat 1 tablespoon oil in a high-sided cooking pot or flameproof casserole and add the rice, stirring with a wooden spoon to make sure the rice is well coated with oil. Add the measured hot water and bring to the boil. Cover and leave to simmer gently over low heat for about 15 minutes.

While the rice is cooking, heat a lightly oiled frying pan over a medium heat, add the chopped onion, season with salt and pepper, and sprinkle with thyme. Soften the onion, keeping your eye on the pan to make sure it doesn't burn.

Crumble the Gorgonzola into the bowl of an electric blender, add the milk and fried onion and process to obtain a fine, creamy texture.

Pour the mixture into a small, heavy-bottomed pan, cover and reheat gently for 8–10 minutes.

Separate the grains of rice with a fork and serve with the Gorgonzola cream, sprinkled with chopped parsley.

Pilau rice with almonds and pine nuts

Serves 4
Preparation: 5 minutes
Cooking: 20 minutes

175 g/6 oz/generous ³/4 cup long-grain rice, washed and drained
300 ml/¹/2 pint/1¹/4 cups hot water
100 g/3¹/2 oz/²/3 cup pine nuts
100 g/3¹/2 oz/²/3 cup almonds
1 tablespoon oil, for cooking
salt and freshly ground black pepper

Heat 1 tablespoon oil in a high-sided cooking pot or flameproof casserole and add the rice, stirring with a wooden spoon to make sure the rice is well coated with oil.

Add the measured hot water to the pan and season with salt and pepper. Bring to the boil, cover and leave to simmer gently over low heat for about 15 minutes.

While the rice is cooking, lightly toast the pine nuts and then the almonds in a dry frying pan.

Separate the grains of rice with a fork and serve with the toasted nuts.

Lemon coconut rice

Serves 4
Preparation: 5 minutes
Cooking: 20 minutes

175 g/6 oz/generous ³/4 cup basmati rice
300 ml/¹/2 pint/1¹/4 cups hot water
juice of 1 lemon
1 cinnamon stick
pinch of sugar
40 g/1¹/2 oz/¹/2 cup grated coconut
oil, for cooking
salt

Rinse the rice in cold running water until the water runs clear and then drain through a sieve or strainer. Turn into a pan and add the measured hot water, lemon juice, cinnamon stick and sugar. Bring to the boil, cover and leave to simmer gently over low heat for about 15 minutes.

Heat a lightly oiled frying pan over medium heat, add the grated coconut and fry lightly, stirring continuously with a wooden spoon.

Just before serving, fluff up the grains of rice with a fork and top with the fried coconut. You can also break the cinnamon stick into four and use to decorate the rice.

Pilau rice with chanterelle mushrooms

Serves 4
Preparation: 15 minutes
Cooking: 20 minutes

250 g/8 oz chanterelle mushrooms
2 shallots, peeled and chopped
175 g/6 oz/generous ³/4 cup long-grain rice, washed and drained
300 ml/¹/2 pint/1¹/4 cups chicken stock
2 tablespoons chopped flat-leaf parsley
butter, for cooking
oil, for cooking
salt and freshly ground black pepper

Carefully clean the mushrooms by rinsing under the cold tap, draining and blotting gently dry with kitchen paper.

Heat 1 tablespoon oil in a high-sided cooking pot or flameproof casserole and lightly fry the shallots over medium heat. Then add the rice, stirring with a wooden spoon so that the grains are well coated with oil.

Add the chicken stock to the rice, bring to the boil, cover and leave to simmer gently over low heat for about 15 minutes.

Heat a knob of butter in a frying pan and fry the mushrooms over medium heat for a few minutes. Season with salt and pepper and add the chopped parsley.

Fluff up the grains of rice with a fork and serve with the sautéed mushrooms.

Persian-style crispy rice

For this recipe you'll need a very heavy-botto-med pan and lots of patience as you have to "burn" the rice without ruining the pan. So, be warned.

Serves 4–6
Preparation: 15 minutes
Cooking: 45 minutes
Soaking: 3 hours

500 g/1 lb/2¾ cups basmati rice
4½ tablespoons butter
pinch of saffron
salt

Rinse the rice under cold running water until the water runs clear, then leave to soak in a bowl of water for about 3 hours. Drain well.

Bring a large pan of salted water to the boil and add the rice. Leave to cook for about 5 minutes and drain. Check the rice – the grains should be tender on the outside but still firm on the inside.

Melt the butter in a heavy-bottomed high-sided cooking pot or flameproof casserole which has a tight-fitting lid and add the rice. Mix well, cover and leave to cook over medium heat for about 15 minutes. Reduce the heat and continue cooking over *very* low heat for another 20 minutes.

Mix a pinch of saffron with 2 tablespoons hot water. Fill a small bowl with rice from the cooking pot and add the flavoured saffron water.

Turn the rest of the rice onto a serving dish and top with a dome of the saffron rice. Use a wooden spoon to remove the crispy rice still attached to the bottom of the pot and serve separately in a small dish.

Diced beef with onion

Serves 4
Preparation: 15 minutes
Cooking: 10 minutes

250 g/8 oz/1¼ cups long-grain rice, already cooked and set aside
400 g/14 oz beef fillet or entrecote steak
2 tablespoons light soy sauce
4 onions
pinch of paprika
oil, for cooking
salt and freshly ground black pepper

Cut the beef into cubes, cover with soy sauce and mix well. Peel and chop the onions.

Heat 1 tablespoon oil in a frying pan over medium heat and quick-fry the diced beef. Season with salt and pepper, turn into a dish and keep warm.

Lightly fry the chopped onions in the frying pan used for the beef, add the cooked rice, sprinkle with paprika and cook for a few minutes over medium heat, stirring continuously with a wooden spoon.

Serve the rice very hot with the diced beef.

Diced sesame chicken

Serves 4
Preparation: 5 minutes
Cooking: 20 minutes

175 g/6 oz/generous ¾ cup long-grain rice, washed and drained
300 ml/½ pint/1¼ cups hot water
500 g/1 lb boned skinless chicken breasts
4–5 tablespoons sesame seeds
oil, for cooking
salt and freshly ground black pepper

Heat 1 tablespoon oil in a heavy-bottomed pan and add the rice, stirring with a wooden spoon so that the grains are well coated with oil. Then add the measured hot water and season with salt and pepper. Bring to the boil, cover and leave to simmer gently over low heat for about 15 minutes.

Cut the chicken breasts into even-sized cubes and season with salt and pepper. Put the sesame seeds into a dish and coat the chicken with seeds.

Heat a lightly oiled frying pan or wok and cook the chicken over medium heat for 4–5 minutes, stirring continuously to make sure it is well browned on all sides.

Fluff up the grains of rice with a fork and serve with the diced sesame chicken.

Rice cooked in red wine, with sautéed beef

Serves 4
Preparation: 15 minutes
Cooking: 20 minutes

100 ml/3½ fl oz/scant ½ cup light red wine
200 ml/7 fl oz/¾ cup chicken stock
2 shallots
175g/6 oz/generous ¾ cup long-grain rice, washed and drained
2 sprigs fresh thyme
625 g/1¼ lb beef fillet or entrecote steak, sliced
4 tablespoons chopped flat-leaf parsley
oil, for cooking
salt and freshly ground black pepper

Preheat the oven to 180°C (350°F), gas mark 4.

Heat the wine and chicken stock in a pan.

Peel and chop the shallots. Heat 1 tablespoon oil in a high-sided cooking pot or flameproof casserole, add the shallots and fry lightly over medium heat until transparent, stirring from time to time. Add the rice and mix well so that the grains are well coated with oil. Pour on the wine and stock, season with salt and pepper, and add the thyme. Bring to the boil, cover and cook in the oven for about 15 minutes. Remove the thyme sprigs.

Cut the beef into thin strips about 6 cm/2½ inches long. Heat a lightly oiled frying pan and quick-fry the strips of beef.

Fluff up the grains of rice with a fork and serve hot with the sautéed beef.

Pilau rice with lime

Serves 4
Preparation: 10 minutes
Cooking: 15 minutes

175 g/6 oz/generous ¾ cup long-grain rice,
washed and drained
300 ml/½ pint/1¼ cups hot water
2 ripe avocados
pinch of mild chilli powder
½ onion, peeled and finely chopped
2 tablespoons chopped fresh coriander leaves
(cilantro)
juice of 2 limes
oil, for cooking
salt and freshly ground black pepper

Preheat the oven to 200°C (400°F), gas mark 6.

Heat 1 tablespoon oil in a high-sided cooking pot
or flameproof casserole and add the rice, stirring
with a wooden spoon so that the grains are well
coated in oil.

Add the measured hot water and season with
salt. Bring to the boil, cover and leave to simmer
gently over low heat for about 15 minutes.

While the rice is cooking, peel the avocados, cut
the flesh into small pieces and mash to a purée
with a fork. Add the chilli powder, onion and
chopped coriander leaves. Season with salt and
pepper, add the juice of 1 lime and mix well.

Fluff up the grains of rice with a fork and sprinkle
with the rest of the lime juice just before serving.
Serve with the avocado purée.

Rice with leeks, ginger and cumin

Serves 4
Preparation: 10 minutes
Cooking: 10 minutes

250 g/8 oz/1¼ cups long-grain rice, already
cooked and set aside
2 medium-sized leeks
1 teaspoon grated fresh ginger
1 teaspoon ground cumin
olive oil, for cooking
salt and freshly ground black pepper

Discard the tough or damaged outer leaves from
the leeks, wash, blot dry with kitchen paper and
slice thinly.

Heat 1 tablespoon oil in a large frying pan. Add
the grated ginger, stirring with a wooden spoon,
then the cumin and sliced leeks. Season with salt
and pepper and cook over medium heat for about
10 minutes, stirring continuously. If necessary,
add 1–2 tablespoons water to prevent the leeks
sticking to the bottom of the pan. Add the
cooked rice, using a fork to fluff up the grains.

Serve hot.

Sage-steamed rice

Serves 4–6
Preparation: 5 minutes, 1 hour in advance
Cooking: 20 minutes

200 g/7 oz/1 cup long-grain rice, washed
and drained
4 sage leaves
salt and freshly ground black pepper

Place the washed rice in a large bowl and cover
with cold water. Leave to soak for at least 1 hour
and then drain.

Fill the bottom part of a steamer with water,
add the sage leaves and bring to the boil. Place
the rice in the perforated container or basket
preferably lined with a piece of muslin (see basic
recipe for steamed rice on page 12), cover with
a tight-fitting lid and leave to cook for about
20 minutes. If you have lined the steamer
container with muslin, don't forget to remove
the lid and leave the rice to stand for a minute
when it is cooked.

Season with salt and pepper and serve hot.

Rice with lemon, basil and parsley

Serves 4–6
Preparation: 10 minutes
Cooking: 20 minutes

2 untreated lemons
175 g/6 oz/generous ¾ cup long-grain rice,
washed and drained
300 ml/½ pint/1¼ cups chicken stock
4 tablespoons chopped fresh basil
4 tablespoons chopped flat-leaf parsley
oil, for cooking
salt and freshly ground black pepper
50 g/1¾ oz/½ cup freshly grated Parmesan
cheese

Rinse and dry the lemons and grate the rind.

Heat 1 tablespoon oil in a high-sided cooking pot
or flameproof casserole, add the rice and fry
lightly over medium heat, stirring continuously so
that the grains are well coated with oil.

Heat the chicken stock in a pan and pour over the
rice. Add the basil, parsley, and grated lemon
rind. Season with salt and pepper, cover and leave
to cook for about 15 minutes over low heat. Fluff
up the grains of rice with a fork.

Serve hot with the grated Parmesan.

SALADS

Goat's cheese and walnut salad

Serves 4
Preparation: 10 minutes
Cooking: 15 minutes

125 g/4 oz/generous ½ cup long-grain rice,
washed and drained
1 small round or about 75 g/3 oz (dryish)
goat's cheese
1 tablespoon white wine vinegar
1 tablespoon tapenade*
3 tablespoons olive oil
grated rind of 1 lemon
1 endive (chicory or escarole) heart
handful of shelled walnuts
1 tablespoon chopped fresh chives
salt and freshly ground black pepper

* A purée of pitted black olives, capers, herbs
and anchovies with added olive oil and lemon
juice (Provence, France).

Make Creole rice by cooking it for 15 minutes in
plenty of water (see recipe page 10). The rice
should be tender but still have a bit of bite (al
dente). Drain through a sieve or strainer and rinse
under cold running water to stop it cooking, then
leave to cool while draining.

Remove the rind from the goat's cheese and cut
into flakes.

To make the vinaigrette, mix the wine vinegar
with the tapenade, season lightly with salt and
whisk vigorously. Add the oil a little at a time,
mix in the grated lemon rind, and season with
black pepper.

Turn the rice into a large serving dish and add
the endive leaves, walnuts, flaked goat's cheese,
chopped chives and lemon vinaigrette. Season
with salt and pepper.

Provençal mesclun with pine nuts

Serves 4
Preparation: 10 minutes
Cooking: 15 minutes

125 g/4 oz/generous ½ cup long-grain rice,
washed and drained
50 g/1¾ oz Provençal mesclun (mixed herb salad)
1 dozen cherry tomatoes or 4 medium tomatoes,
quartered
1 small celery stalk, diced
50 g/1¾ oz /½ cup freshly grated Parmesan
2 tablespoons pine nuts
1 tablespoon white wine vinegar
3 tablespoons olive oil
salt and freshly ground black pepper
5 fresh basil leaves, torn into small pieces

Make Creole rice by cooking it for 15 minutes in
plenty of water (see recipe page 10). The rice
should be tender but still have a bit of bite (al
dente). Turn into a sieve or strainer and rinse
under cold running water to stop it cooking,
drain carefully and leave to cool.

Arrange the rice and mesclun leaves in a large
serving dish. Add the tomatoes, diced celery,
grated Parmesan and pine nuts.

To make the vinaigrette, mix the wine vinegar
with a pinch of salt, then add the olive oil, a little
at a time, whisking continuously. Pour over the
salad and sprinkle with the torn basil to serve.

Minty artichoke salad

Serves 4
Preparation: 10 minutes
Cooking: 20 minutes

6 small violet artichokes
juice of 1 lemon
4 fresh mint leaves
125g/4 oz/generous ½ cup long-grain rice,
washed and drained
1 tablespoon white wine vinegar
2 tablespoons sunflower oil
1 teaspoon smooth Dijon mustard
salt and freshly ground black pepper

Remove the outer leaves of the artichokes and
cut off the tops, leaving 2–3 cm/¾–1¼ inches
of the leaves. Cut off the base, remove the choke
(if it has developed) and sprinkle with lemon juice
to prevent discoloration.

Pour some water in the base of a steamer or a
pan, add the mint leaves and bring to the boil.
Place the artichokes in the perforated container,
or basket over a pan of water, cover and leave to
cook for about 20 minutes.

While the artichokes are cooking, make Creole
rice (see recipe page 10). The rice should be
tender but still have a bit of bite (al dente). Turn
into a sieve or strainer and rinse under cold
running water to stop it cooking, drain carefully
and leave to cool.

To make the vinaigrette, pour the wine vinegar
into a bowl, mix in the mustard and season lightly
with salt. Add the sunflower oil, a little at a time,
whisking continuously. Season with black pepper.

Arrange the cold rice and artichokes on a large
serving dish and pour over the vinaigrette.

Chicory (Belgian endive) and walnut salad with cream sauce

Serves 4
Preparation: 10 minutes
Cooking: 15 minutes

125 g/4 oz/generous ½ cup long-grain rice, washed and drained
3 medium-sized heads chicory (Belgian endive)
1 dozen pitted black olives
handful of shelled walnuts
pared zest of 1 untreated orange
2 teaspoons lemon juice
3 tablespoons crème fraîche or plain yogurt
salt and freshly ground black pepper

Make Creole rice by cooking it for 15 minutes in plenty of water (see recipe page 10). The rice should be tender but still have a bit of bite (al dente). Turn into a sieve or strainer and rinse under cold running water to stop it cooking, drain carefully and leave to cool.

Wash the chicory, blot dry with kitchen paper and chop finely. Arrange the rice and chicory on a large serving dish and add the olives, walnuts and the pared strips of orange zest.

Put the lemon juice and crème fraîche, or yogurt, in a bowl, season with salt and pepper, and whisk vigorously.

Just before serving, pour over the cream sauce.

Wild rice salad with smoked salmon

Serves 4
Preparation: 10 minutes
Cooking: 45 minutes

300 ml/½ pint/1¼ cups water
125 g/4 oz/generous ½ cup wild rice, washed and drained
½ teaspoon smooth Dijon mustard
1 tablespoon cider vinegar
3 tablespoons sunflower oil
1 tablespoon maple syrup
1 tablespoon dark soy sauce
200 g/7 oz smoked salmon, cut into thin strips
salt and freshly ground black pepper
1 tablespoon sesame seeds, toasted

Bring the measured water to the boil in a large pan. Season with salt, add the rice and stir well. Cover and leave to simmer gently over low heat for 45 minutes.

The rice should be tender but still have a bit of bite (al dente). Turn into a sieve or strainer and rinse under the cold tap to stop it cooking, drain carefully and leave to cool.

To make the vinaigrette, mix the mustard with the cider vinegar, sunflower oil, maple syrup and soy sauce. Season to taste with salt and pepper.

Turn the wild rice into a serving dish, top with strips of smoked salmon and pour over the vinaigrette dressing.

Serve sprinkled with toasted sesame seeds and seasoned with black pepper.

Citrus rice salad

Serves 4
Preparation: 15 minutes
Cooking: 15 minutes

125 g/4 oz/generous ½ cup long-grain rice, washed and drained
1 orange
1 grapefruit
6 tablespoons orange juice
5 tablespoons grapefruit juice
1 tablespoon clear honey
2 tablespoons sunflower oil
1 teaspoon grated fresh ginger
1 tablespoon chopped fresh mixed herbs (chives, parsley, tarragon, chervil…)
1 dozen shelled pistachio nuts
salt and freshly ground black pepper

Make Creole rice by cooking it for 15 minutes in plenty of water (see recipe page 10). The rice should be tender but still have a bit of bite (al dente). Turn into a sieve or strainer and rinse under cold running water to stop it cooking, drain carefully and leave to cool.

Peel the orange and grapefruit, remove the pith and roughly chop the flesh, removing any pips. Turn the rice into a large serving dish and add the orange and grapefruit pieces.

To make the vinaigrette, whisk the orange and grapefruit juice together with the clear honey and sunflower oil. Season with salt and pepper, and stir in the grated ginger.

Pour the vinaigrette over the rice salad, sprinkle with the chopped mixed herbs and decorate with the pistachio nuts.

Sun-dried and cherry tomatoes with balsamic vinegar

Serves 4
Preparation: 10 minutes
Cooking: 15 minutes

300 ml/$\frac{1}{2}$ pint/1$\frac{1}{4}$ cups water
125 g/4 oz/generous $\frac{1}{2}$ cup long-grain rice,
washed and drained
12 cherry tomatoes
100 g/3$\frac{1}{2}$ oz/$\frac{3}{4}$ cup sun-dried tomatoes, in oil
10 small pitted black olives
1 small, red salad onion
5 fresh basil leaves
1 tablespoon balsamic vinegar
1 teaspoon smooth Dijon mustard
3 tablespoons basil-flavoured olive oil
100 g/3$\frac{1}{2}$ oz/1$\frac{1}{3}$ cups mangetout (snow peas),
already cooked
salt and freshly ground black pepper

Bring the measured water to the boil in a large pan, season with salt, add the rice and stir well. Cover, reduce to low heat, and leave to simmer gently for about 15 minutes. The rice should be tender but still have a bit of a bite (al dente). Turn into a sieve or strainer and rinse under cold running water to stop it cooking, drain and leave to cool.

Rinse the cherry tomatoes and blot dry with kitchen paper. Drain the oil from the sun-dried tomatoes and cut into thin strips. Rinse and drain the olives, peel and thinly slice the salad onion, rinse and tear the basil leaves into small pieces.

To make the vinaigrette, mix the balsamic vinegar and mustard in a bowl and season with salt. Add the olive oil, a little at a time, whisking vigorously.

Put the rice, mangetout, cherry tomatoes and strips of sun-dried tomato into a serving dish. Add the sliced onion, basil and black olives and pour over the vinaigrette. Season generously with black pepper.

Serve well chilled.

Fennel and apple salad

Serves 4
Preparation: 15 minutes
Cooking: 12 minutes

300 ml/¹/₂ pint/1¹/₄ cups water
125 g/4 oz/generous ¹/₂ cup long-grain rice,
washed and drained
2 small fennel bulbs
3 sharp apples (Granny Smith, Cox's, Braeburn...)
juice of 1 lime
salt

Bring the measured water to the boil in a large
pan and season with salt. Add the rice and stir
well. Cover, reduce to low heat, and leave to
simmer gently for about 12 minutes.

The rice should be tender but still with a bit of
bite (al dente). Turn into a sieve or strainer and
rinse under cold running water to stop it cooking,
drain carefully and leave to cool.

Rinse the fennel, cut the bulbs into four and then
each quarter into small cubes. Peel, core, and
quarter the apples – cut each quarter into small
cubes. Sprinkle the apple and fennel with lime
juice to stop discoloration.

Turn the rice into a bowl and top with the diced
apple and fennel.

Apple, pear and walnut salad

Serves 4
Preparation: 10 minutes
Cooking: 15 minutes

300 ml/¹/₂ pint/1¹/₄ cups water
125 g/4 oz/generous ¹/₂ cup long-grain rice,
washed and drained
2 sharp apples (Granny Smith, Cox's, Braeburn...)
2 pears
juice and grated rind of 1 untreated lemon
1 teaspoon wholegrain mustard
1 tablespoon cider vinegar
1 tablespoon walnut oil
2 tablespoons sunflower oil
handful of shelled walnuts
salt and freshly ground black pepper

Bring the measured water to the boil in a large
pan and season with salt. Add the rice and stir
well. Cover, reduce to low heat, and leave to
simmer gently for about 15 minutes.

The rice should be tender but still have a bit of
bite (al dente). Turn into a sieve or strainer and
rinse under cold running water to stop it cooking,
drain and leave to cool.

Peel, core, and quarter the apples and pears. Cut
into small cubes and sprinkle with lemon juice to
stop discoloration.

To make the vinaigrette, mix the mustard with
the cider vinegar, season lightly with salt and
gradually whisk in the 2 oils, a little at a time.
Season with black pepper.

Put the rice, diced apple and pear, and walnuts in
a large serving dish. Top with grated lemon rind
and pour over the vinaigrette.

Feta cheese and Kalamata olives with vinaigrette

Serves 4
Preparation: 10 minutes
Cooking: 15 minutes

300 ml/¹/₂ pint/1¹/₄ cups water
125 g/4 oz/generous ¹/₂ cup long-grain rice,
washed and drained
4 tomatoes
1 white onion
1 garlic clove
200 g/7 oz feta cheese
20 pitted Kalamata (Greek black) olives
1 tablespoon capers, in vinegar
4 tablespoons chopped flat-leaf parsley
1 tablespoon white wine vinegar
3 tablespoons olive oil
pinch of dried thyme
salt and freshly ground black pepper
To serve: a few fresh basil leaves, rinsed and
torn into small pieces

Bring the measured water to the boil in a large
pan and season with salt. Add the rice and stir
well. Cover, reduce to a low heat, and leave to
simmer gently for about 15 minutes.

The rice should be tender but still have a bit of
bite (al dente). Turn into a sieve or strainer and
rinse under cold running water to stop it cooking,
drain carefully and leave to cool.

Rinse the tomatoes, blot dry with kitchen paper
and chop roughly. Peel and chop the onion and
garlic clove. Cut the feta into small cubes, and the
olives into thin strips. Drain the capers.

Turn the rice into a large serving dish and top
with the tomatoes, onion, garlic, feta cheese,
olives, capers and chopped parsley.

To make the vinaigrette, mix the wine vinegar
with a pinch of salt and gradually whisk in the
olive oil, a little at a time. Add the thyme and
pour over the salad. Season with black pepper.

Sprinkle with the pieces of basil leaf just before
serving.

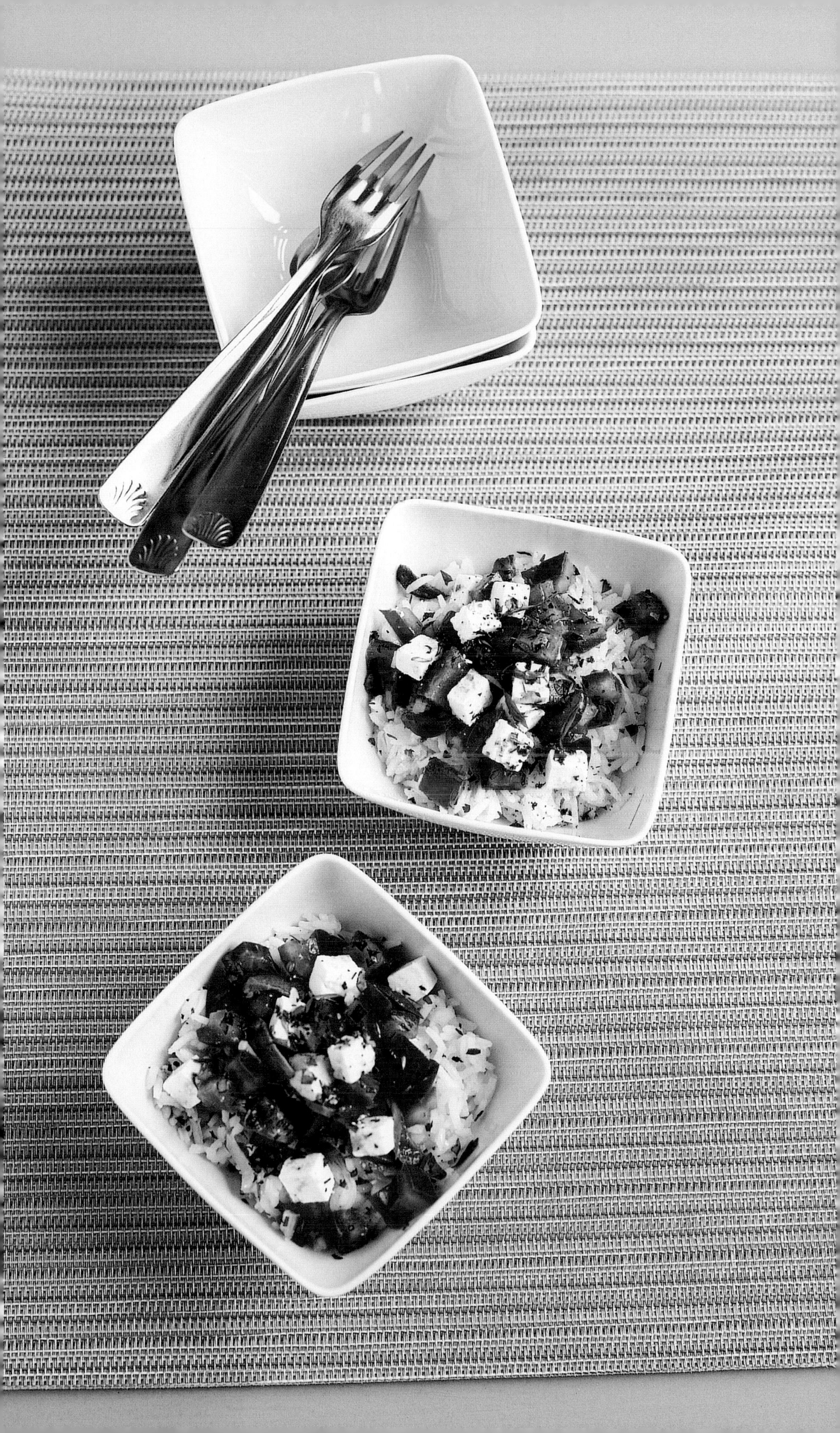

SNACKS AND APPETIZERS

Coconut-rice bites

Serves 4–6
Preparation: 5 minutes, 1 hour in advance
Cooking: 8 minutes

200 g/7 oz/1 cup sticky rice
125 ml/4 fl oz/½ cup coconut milk
pinch of salt

Put the rice in a large bowl or pan, cover with water and leave to soak for at least 1 hour. Drain well and place in the centre of a clean tea cloth or piece of muslin or cheesecloth.

Pour some water in the base of a steamer, or in a pan, and bring to the boil. Place the cloth or muslin containing the rice in the perforated container of the steamer, or in a basket over a pan, fold in the edges, cover and leave to cook for 8–10 minutes.

Remove from the heat and remove the lid of the steamer, open up the cloth and allow the rice to cool for a minute before turning into a large bowl.

Add the coconut milk, season with salt and mix well. The rice should be served warm.

Pack the rice into small coffee cups or other variously shaped containers of about the same size. Turn out onto small plates and serve as an accompaniment or just eat with your fingers.

Vietnamese prawn (shrimp) and chicken rolls

Serves 4
Preparation: 25 minutes
Cooking: 3 minutes

30 g/1 oz rice noodles
200 g/7 oz uncooked prawns (shrimp), peeled
200 g/7 oz boned skinless chicken breasts
1 carrot, peeled and grated
1 garlic clove, peeled and chopped
1 tablespoon coconut, grated
12 rice pancakes
oil, for cooking
salt and freshly ground black pepper
To serve: a few fresh lettuce leaves, fresh mint, spicy dipping sauce.

Cook the rice noodles according to the instructions on the packet. Chop the prawns and chicken, and place into a large bowl with the cooked and drained rice noodles, carrot, garlic and coconut. Season with salt and pepper and mix well.

Dip each pancake into a bowl of water to which a little sugar has been added, leave just long enough to soften, then blot dry with kitchen paper. Lay the pancakes on a work surface and place some of the filling in the centre of each. Fold in the side nearest you, then the left and right sides of the pancake and roll towards the remaining edge.

Fry the rolls in very hot oil and drain well on kitchen paper. Serve warm with lettuce leaves, fresh mint and spicy dipping sauce.

Vietnamese chicken rolls

Serves 4
Preparation: 35 minutes
Cooking: 5 minutes
Soaking: 30 minutes

4 dried cloud ears (Chinese black mushrooms) (see note)
40 g/1½ oz rice noodles
200 g/7 oz pork fillet or tenderloin, chopped
200 g/7 oz boned skinless chicken breast, chopped
1 carrot, peeled and grated
1 garlic clove, peeled and chopped
1 teaspoon fresh ginger, grated
1 tablespoon de nuoc-mâm*
12 rice pancakes
oil, for cooking
freshly ground black pepper
To serve: a few fresh lettuce leaves, fresh mint, spicy dipping sauce.

*A condiment used in Vietnamese cookery that tends to replace salt in most dishes. It is a paste made by pounding small fish marinated in brine.

Soak the cloud ear mushrooms in a bowl of warm water for about 30 minutes. Drain, blot dry with kitchen paper and chop.

Cook the rice noodles according to the instructions on the packet. Put the pork, chicken, cooked and drained rice noodles, mushrooms, carrot, garlic, ginger and nuoc-mâm in a large bowl. Season with salt and pepper and mix well.

Dip each pancake into a bowl of water to which a little sugar has been added, leave just long enough to soften, then blot dry with kitchen paper. Lay the pancakes on a work surface and place some of the filling in the centre of each. Fold in the side nearest you, then the left and right sides of the pancake and roll towards the remaining edge.

Fry the rolls in very hot oil and leave to drain on kitchen paper. Serve warm with lettuce leaves, fresh mint and spicy dipping sauce.

Note: cloud ears (Chinese Black mushrooms) can be found in Chinese and Oriental stores. They are dried and must be reconstituted.

Spring rolls

Serves 4
Preparation: 25 minutes
Cooking: 3 minutes

40 g/1½ oz rice noodles
50 g/1¾ oz/⅔ cup fresh bean sprouts
a few fresh lettuce leaves, shredded
12 rice pancakes
150 g/5 oz /1 loosely packed cup peeled and grated carrots
200 g/7 oz prawns (shrimp), cooked and peeled
2 tablespoons chopped fresh mint
1 tablespoon chopped fresh coriander leaves (cilantro)
a few fresh chive stems
To serve: spicy dipping sauce, if desired

Cook the rice noodles according to the instructions on the packet. Rinse the bean sprouts and lettuce leaves, then dry, in a salad spinner if possible.

Dip each rice pancake into a bowl of water to which a little sugar has been added, leave just long enough to soften, then blot dry with kitchen paper. Lay the pancakes on a work surface and place a little grated carrot and rice noodles, a few prawns and bean sprouts and a little chopped mint and coriander in the centre of each. Fold in the side nearest you, then the left and right sides of the pancake and roll towards the remaining edge, slipping a chive stem into each roll.

Fry the rolls in very hot oil and leave to drain on kitchen paper. Serve warm with a spicy dipping sauce, mild or hot, depending on your taste.

Japanese sushi rolls

Roll your own sushi by spreading sushi rice on a sheet of nori seaweed, adding a touch of wasabi paste and a little filling, and rolling the nori into a cone shape. Dark soy sauce makes an ideal dipping sauce.

Sushi rice

Serves 4
Preparation: 30 minutes
Cooking: 15 minutes
Draining: at least 30 minutes

200 g/7 oz/1 cup short-grain white sushi rice
250 ml/8 fl oz/1 cup water
5–6 tablespoons rice vinegar
2 tablespoons sugar
1/2 teaspoon salt
6 sheets dried nori seaweed, about 18 x 20 cm/
7 x 8 inches

Put the rice in a large bowl, cover with cold water and mix with your fingers. Drain and repeat two or three times until the water is clear. Leave to drain in a sieve or strainer for at least 30 minutes.

Put the rice and measured water into a small pan and bring to the boil. Reduce the heat, cover and leave to cook over low heat for about 12 minutes. Remove from the heat and leave to stand, without removing the lid, for 10–15 minutes.

Mix the rice vinegar, sugar and salt in a bowl. Spread the warm rice on a large serving dish, drizzle with the vinegar seasoning and mix well. If necessary, add a little more vinegar mixture. Cover with a clean, damp cloth and leave to cool.

Lightly toast the nori by waving it over a hot flame for a few seconds, until it begins to change colour and becomes fragrant, or according to the packet instructions. Cut each sheet into 4 with scissors.

The rice and nori can be used to prepare one of the following sushi recipes.

Note. The red pickled ginger (*gari* or *beni-shoga*) used in the recipes is available in Japanese stores.

Fish-roe sushi

200 g/7 oz fresh cod or salmon roe
Japanese soy sauce (*shoyu*)
wasabi paste
red pickled ginger (*gari* or *beni-shoga*)
a few fresh basil leaves

Arrange sheets of nori and fish roe on a serving dish and place the rice in a separate bowl.

Serve with the shoyu, wasabi paste, pickled ginger and basil leaves in individual dishes.

Vegetarian sushi

1 cucumber
Japanese soy sauce (*shoyu*)
wasabi paste
red pickled ginger (*gari* or *beni-shoga*)
1 dozen fresh basil leaves
2 tablespoons sesame seeds, toasted

Rinse the cucumber, slice in half from top to bottom, then cut into thin strips about 4 cm/ 1½ inches long.

Arrange sheets of nori and strips of cucumber on a serving dish and place the rice in a separate bowl.

Serve with the shoyu, wasabi paste, pickled ginger, basil leaves and sesame seeds in individual dishes.

Salmon and dill sushi

250 g/8 oz smoked salmon
Japanese dark soy sauce (*shoyu*) (not Chinese – the Japanese variety is lighter and sweeter)
wasabi paste
red pickled ginger (*gari* or *beni-shoga*)
a few sprigs fresh dill

Cut the smoked salmon into thin strips. Arrange sheets of nori and strips of salmon on a serving dish and place the rice in a separate bowl.

Serve with the shoyu, wasabi paste, pickled ginger and sprigs of dill in individual dishes.

Avocado and crab sushi

1 avocado
juice of 1 lemon
100 g/3½ oz crab meat, cooked and shelled
Japanese soy sauce (*shoyu*)
wasabi paste
red pickled ginger (*gari* or *beni-shoga*)

Peel and thinly slice the avocado, and sprinkle with lemon juice to prevent discoloration.

Arrange sheets of nori, sliced avocado and crab meat on a serving dish and place the rice in a separate bowl.

Serve with the shoyu, wasabi paste and pickled ginger in individual dishes.

Stuffed vine leaves

Serves 4–6
Preparation: 35 minutes
Cooking: 45 minutes

300 g/10 oz/1¼ cups minced (ground) lamb
3 fresh mint leaves, finely chopped
1 bunch flat-leaf parsley, finely chopped
finely grated rind of 1 lemon
1 onion
1 tablespoon olive oil
200 g/7 oz/1 cup short-grain rice, washed
and drained
250 g/8 oz vine leaves (grape leaves)
3 garlic cloves, peeled
1 litre/1¾ pints/4 cups warm vegetable stock
juice of 2 lemons
pinch ground cinnamon
salt and freshly ground black pepper

Put the lamb, mint leaves, parsley and grated lemon rind in a bowl, season generously with salt and pepper, and mix well.

Peel and finely chop the onion.

Heat the olive oil in a frying pan and lightly fry the onion over medium heat until transparent. Add the rice and cook until transparent, then add the lamb mixture. Mix well and cook for another 5 minutes or so.

Rinse and drain the vine leaves according to the instructions on the packaging. Blot dry with kitchen paper and spread out on a flat work surface.

Place a small amount of filling in the centre of each leaf, fold in the stalk side first, then the left and right sides and roll tightly towards the remaining edge. Fill and roll all the leaves in the same way.

Arrange the stuffed vine leaves in a high-sided cooking pot or flameproof casserole. Add the garlic cloves and cover with warm stock, adding a little water if necessary. When the stock begins to simmer, cover and cook gently over low heat for about 40 minutes.

Add the lemon juice and cinnamon, and cook for another 8–10 minutes.

Serve warm.

Prawn (shrimp) and coconut bites

Serves 4–6
Preparation: 15 minutes
Cooking: 20 minutes

175 g/6 oz/generous ¾ cup long-grain rice,
washed and drained
300 ml/½ pint/1¼ cups water
1.5 litres/2½ pints/6 cups coconut milk
grated rind of 1 untreated lemon
400 g/14 oz uncooked prawns (shrimp), peeled
1 teaspoon fresh ginger, chopped
1 egg yolk
1 slice white bread, broken into pieces
1 teaspoon cornflour (cornstarch)
salt and freshly ground black pepper

Place the rice in a heavy-bottomed pan, add the
measured water, season with salt and pepper,
and bring to the boil. Cover, reduce the heat and
leave to cook over low heat for about 15 minutes.

Put the coconut milk and grated lemon rind in a
large, heavy-bottomed pan, season with pepper
and bring to the boil.

Roughly chop the prawns and place in the bowl
of an electric blender. Add the ginger, egg yolk,
bread and cornflour, season lightly with pepper
and process to a fine consistency. Then use your
hands to shape the mixture into even-sized balls.

Place the balls in the pan of coconut milk and
leave to simmer gently for about 8 minutes.

After 15 minutes remove the rice pan from the
heat and leave to stand, without removing the
lid, for about 10 minutes. Then fluff up the rice
by stirring with a fork.

Drain the prawn balls and serve immediately.

WOK, WOK, WOK

Stir-fried beef with orange zest

Serves 4
Preparation: 20 minutes
Cooking: 15 minutes

400 g/14 oz beef fillet, or entrecote, steak
3 tablespoons soy sauce
rind pared from an untreated orange, with
a zester
175 g/6 oz/generous 3/4 cup long-grain rice,
washed and drained
3 large onions, peeled and sliced into rounds
groundnut (peanut) oil, for cooking
salt and freshly ground black pepper

Cut the beef into fine strips about 5-cm/2 inches
long and place on a dish. Pour over the soy sauce,
stir, and cover the dish. Set aside to marinate in
a cool place while the rice cooks.

Cut the orange zest into small strips.

Tip the rice into a heavy-bottomed pan. Pour in
300 ml/1/2 pint/1 1/4 cups water, and add salt and
pepper to taste. Bring to the boil, cover, reduce
the heat and cook for about 15 minutes. Remove
the pan from the heat and leave covered and
undisturbed for about 10 minutes. Fluff up the
rice with chopsticks.

Drain the beef. Heat 1 tablespoon oil in the wok.
Add the meat and stir-fry over fairly high heat,
then remove from wok, set aside and keep warm.

Stir-fry the onions in the wok. Add the orange
zest, stir well, then add the reserved beef. Season
to taste and cook for another minute.

Serve immediately with plain rice.

Five-flavour pork

Serves 4
Preparation: 20 minutes
Cooking: 15 minutes

1/2 red bell pepper, sliced thinly
400 g/14 oz pork fillet (tenderloin), cubed
1 teaspoon five-spice powder
200 g/7 oz/1 cup long-grain rice, already
cooked and set aside
groundnut (peanut) oil, for cooking
salt and freshly ground black pepper

Heat 1 tablespoon oil in the wok. Add the red
pepper and stir-fry for 1 minute. Add the cubed
pork and brown over high heat for another
2 minutes. Season with salt and pepper, and
sprinkle with the five-spice powder. Add the
rice, lower the heat and stir-fry for another 2 or
3 minutes. Serve at once.

Note: This recipe can be made with curry
powder instead of the five-spice powder.

Prawns (shrimp) with ginger

Serves 4
Preparation: 10 minutes
Cooking: 15 minutes

175 g/6 oz/generous 3/4 cup long-grain rice,
washed and drained
2 pinches chilli powder
12 large prawns (shrimp)
2 onions, chopped
1 garlic clove, chopped
1 teaspoon freshly grated ginger
2 pinches turmeric
oil, for cooking
salt and freshly ground black pepper

Tip the rice into a heavy-bottomed pan. Pour in
300 ml/1/2 pint/1 1/4 cups water. Add 1 pinch chilli
powder and season with salt and pepper. Bring
to the boil, cover, reduce the heat and cook for
about 15 minutes. Remove the pan from the
heat and leave covered and undisturbed for about
10 minutes. Fluff up the rice with chopsticks.

Peel the prawns.

Heat 1 tablespoon oil in a wok or frying pan.
Stir-fry the onion, garlic and ginger for a minute
or so, then add the turmeric and the remaining
pinch of chilli powder.

Let the spices heat until fragrant, then add the
prawns. Cook for 8 to 10 minutes, stirring to
combine the spices. Season with salt and pepper.

Transfer the prawns to a large bowl and serve
accompanied by the rice.

Beef with ginger and tomato

Serves 4
Preparation: 15 minutes
Cooking: 10 minutes

400 g/14 oz beef fillet, or entrecote, steak
1 teaspoon grated ginger
1 tablespoon tomato purée (paste)
1 pinch caster (superfine) sugar
2 tablespoons soy sauce
250 g/8 oz/1¼ cups long-grain rice, already
cooked and set aside
oil, for cooking
salt and freshly ground black pepper

Cut the beef into thin strips about 5 cm/2 inches long.

Heat 1 tablespoon oil in a wok or frying pan and add the grated ginger. Give it a stir, then add the tomato purée and pinch of sugar.

Tip the beef strips into the pan and cook for 2 or 3 minutes, then add the soy sauce. Lift out and reserve the meat.

Put the rice into the wok and stir-fry for 2 to 3 minutes.

Arrange the strips of meat on top of the rice and serve at once.

Lamb meatballs with white rice

Serves 4 to 6
Preparation: 25 minutes
Cooking: 25 minutes

1 small bunch parsley
625 g/1¼ lb/2¼ cups minced (ground) lamb
2 pinches cinnamon
2 eggs
3 tablespoons pine nuts
2 tablespoons flour
2 onions, peeled and chopped
800 ml/1¼ pints/3¼ cups vegetable stock
juice of 2 oranges, and finely pared rind of
1 orange
200 g/7 oz/1 cup long-grain rice, washed
and drained
oil, for cooking
salt and freshly ground black pepper
1 tablespoon flour

Wash, dry and chop the parsley.

Place the lamb in a large bowl and sprinkle with
the cinnamon. Season with salt and pepper, then
add the eggs, pine nuts, 1 tablespoon flour and
the chopped parsley. Mix well, then shape into
balls of uniform size.

Heat 1 tablespoon oil in a wok and lightly brown
the onions. Add the meatballs, turning them with
a spatula so that they brown on all sides.

Pour over 500 ml/17 fl oz/2 cups of the stock.
Bring to a simmer, season sparingly with salt and
pepper and add the orange juice. Cook over
medium to low heat for about 15 minutes.

In the meantime, prepare the rice: Heat 1 tablespoon oil in a pan and sauté the rice until golden.
Add the remaining stock and season with salt and
pepper. Bring to a simmer, cover, and cook over
medium to low heat for about 15 minutes. Fluff
up the rice with a fork.

Serve the meatballs with the rice, garnished with
the orange rind cut finely into strips.

Vegetable medley with cloud ear mushrooms

Serves 4
Preparation: 20 minutes
Cooking: 20 minutes

6 dried cloud ears (Chinese black mushrooms) (see note)
200 g/7 oz/1 cup long-grain rice, washed and drained
150 g/5 oz extra-fine French (green) beans, washed, topped and tailed
125 g/4 oz broccoli
1 courgette (zucchini), cut into sticks
1 carrot, peeled and cut into sticks
1 teaspoon grated ginger
oil, for cooking
salt and freshly ground black pepper

Place the cloud ears in a bowl and cover with warm water; soak for about 30 minutes.

Put the rice into a heavy-bottomed pan. Pour in 300 ml/½ pint/1¼ cups water and season with salt and pepper. Bring to the boil, cover, lower the heat and cook over medium heat for about 15 minutes. Remove the pan from the heat and leave covered and undisturbed for about 10 minutes. Fluff up the rice with chopsticks.

Cut the beans into 3.5-cm/1½-inch lengths. Break up the broccoli into florets; rinse, and drain.

Carefully drain the cloud ears; remove the stems, and cut the caps into thin strips.

Heat 1 tablespoon oil in a wok. Tip in all the vegetables and stir-fry for about 3 to 4 minutes. Season with salt and pepper, then sprinkle with the grated ginger.

Serve with the rice.

Note: cloud ears (Chinese Black mushrooms) can be found in Chinese and Oriental stores. They are dried and must be reconstituted.

Chicken and saffron pilaf

Serves 4
Preparation: 15 minutes
Cooking: 35 minutes

½ teaspoon powdered saffron
4 garlic cloves, chopped
4 shallots, chopped
1 teaspoon grated ginger
200 g/7 oz/1 cup long-grain basmati rice, rinsed and drained
2 pinches paprika
200 g/7 oz pork fillet (tenderloin), cubed
200 g/7 oz boned skinless chicken breast, cubed
oil, for cooking
salt and freshly ground black pepper

Mix the saffron with 300 ml/½ pint/1¼ cups water, then warm in a small pan.

Heat 1 tablespoon oil in a wok. Add the garlic, shallots, and grated ginger. Stir-fry for 2 minutes, then pour in the rice and sauté until golden. Pour in the saffron water, season with salt and pepper, and sprinkle in the paprika. Bring to a simmer, cover, and cook over low heat for 15 to 20 minutes.

While the rice is cooking, heat a little oil in a frying pan and brown the cubed pork, then the chicken.

Serve the rice hot, garnished with the meat.

Carrots, beansprouts and mangetout (snow peas)

Serves 4
Preparation: 15 minutes
Cooking: 15 minutes

200 g/7 oz/1 cup long-grain rice, rinsed and drained
200 g/7 oz mangetouts (snow peas)
2 carrots
125 g/4 oz/1⅔ cups beansprouts
1 garlic clove, peeled and finely chopped
1 teaspoon grated ginger
3 teaspoons soy sauce
1 pinch caster (superfine) sugar
oil, for cooking
salt and freshly ground black pepper

Tip the rice into a heavy-bottomed pan and add 350 ml/12 fl oz/1½ cups water. Season with salt and pepper, bring to the boil and cover. Lower the heat and cook for about 15 minutes.

Remove pan from the heat and leave covered and undisturbed for about 10 minutes. Fluff up the rice with chopsticks.

Top and tail the mangetouts, stringing them if necessary, rinse, drain, and cut in half. Peel and cut the carrots into matchsticks. Sort through the beansprouts; wash in cold water and drain.

Heat 1 tablespoon oil in a wok. Add the garlic and ginger, followed by the mangetouts, carrots, and beansprouts. Stir-fry for 2 to 3 minutes, then add the soy sauce, sugar, and 5 tablespoons warm water. Cover and simmer for 3 minutes.

Serve the vegetables with the hot rice.

Basic fried rice

Serves 4
Preparation: 10 minutes
Cooking: 5 minutes

175 g/6 oz/generous ¾ cup long-grain rice,
already cooked and set aside
100 g/3½ oz/¾ cup fresh or frozen peas
2 eggs
2 thick slices ham
2 teaspoons soy sauce
oil, for cooking
salt and freshly ground black pepper

Tip the peas into a pan of boiling salted water
and cook for about 5 minutes. (If using frozen,
cook according to packet instructions.) Drain
and refresh under cold running water.

Crack the eggs into a bowl and beat with a fork.
Season sparingly with salt. Make an omelette
turning it out from the pan with a spatula, then
cut into thin strips. Cut the ham into small cubes.

Heat 1 tablespoon oil in a wok, tip in the rice
and heat for 2 minutes. Add the peas, ham and
omelette strips. Pour in the soy sauce, season to
taste, stir to combine and serve.

Prawn (shrimp) fried rice

Serves 4
Preparation: 10 minutes
Cooking: 5 minutes

175 g/6 oz/generous ¾ cup long-grain rice,
already cooked and set aside
80 g/3 oz dried prawns (shrimp)
100 g/3½ oz/¾ cup fresh or frozen peas
2 eggs, beaten
2 chive stalks
1 shallot
125 g/4 oz roast pork, preferably in one piece
2 teaspoons soy sauce
oil, for cooking
salt and freshly ground black pepper

Place the dried prawns in a bowl, cover with
warm water and soak for 15 minutes.

Tip the peas into a pan of boiling salted water
and cook for about 5 minutes. (If using frozen,
cook according to packet instructions.) Drain
and refresh under cold running water.

Make a well-cooked omelette with the eggs and
cut into thin strips. Wash, dry, and finely snip the
chives. Peel and chop the shallot. Cut the roast
pork into small cubes. Drain the prawns.

Heat a little oil in a wok and fry the chopped
shallot until golden brown. Add the cooked rice
and stir-fry for 2 minutes. Add the prawns, pork,
eggs, chives and peas. Stir in the soy sauce and
season with salt and pepper, stir again and serve.

Red bell pepper fried rice

Serves 4
Preparation: 10 minutes
Cooking: 5 minutes

125 g/4 oz/generous ½ cup long-grain rice,
already cooked and set aside
100 g/3½ oz/¾ cup fresh or frozen peas
2 eggs, beaten
2 onions, peeled and chopped
1 shallot, peeled and chopped
½ bell pepper, diced
100 g fresh prawns (shrimp), cooked and peeled
2 teaspoons soy sauce
oil, for cooking
salt and freshly ground black pepper

Tip the peas into a pan of boiling salted water
and cook for about 5 minutes. (If using frozen,
cook according to packet instructions.) Drain
and refresh under cold running water.

Make a well-cooked omelette with the eggs and
cut into thin strips.

Heat 1 tablespoon oil in a wok and sauté the
onions and shallot until golden brown. Add the
diced pepper and cook for a further minute.
Tip in the rice and stir-fry for 2 minutes. Add the
prawns, peas and the strips of omelette, followed
by the soy sauce. Season to taste, stir and serve.

Sausage fried rice

Serves 4
Preparation: 10 minutes
Cooking: 5 minutes

125 g/4 oz/generous ½ cup long-grain rice,
already cooked and set aside
125 g/4 oz broccoli
100 g/3½ oz/¾ cup fresh or frozen peas
2 eggs, beaten
2 smoked sausages
2 chive stalks, chopped
2 teaspoons soy sauce
oil, for cooking
salt and freshly ground black pepper

Break up the broccoli into florets and rinse. Blanch
for 4 minutes in a pan of boiling salted water.
Refresh under cold running water and drain.

Tip the peas into a pan of boiling salted water
and cook for about 5 minutes. (If using frozen,
cook according to packet instructions.) Drain
and refresh under cold running water.

Make a well-cooked omelette with the eggs and
cut into thin strips. Slice the sausages into rounds.
Wash, dry, and finely snip the chives.

Heat 1 tablespoon oil in a wok, tip in the rice and
stir-fry for 2 minutes. Add the sausage, omelette,
broccoli, peas and chives. Stir in the soy sauce,
season with salt and pepper, stir again and serve.

PATIENCE...

Patience...

Risotto with Parmesan cheese

Serves 4
Preparation: 5 minutes
Cooking: 25 minutes

1 litre/1¾ pints/4 cups chicken stock
2 shallots, peeled and chopped
200 g/7 oz/1 cup superfine Arborio or superfine
Carnaroli rice, washed and drained
3½ tablespoons dry white wine
40 g/1½ oz/⅓ cup freshly grated Parmesan
cheese
1½ tablespoons butter
olive oil, for cooking
salt and freshly ground black pepper

Gently heat the chicken stock in a pan.

Heat 2 tablespoons olive oil in a heavy-bottomed
pan. Add the shallots and sweat for 2 minutes.

Tip in the rice and sauté for a minute or so,
stirring with a wooden spoon until the grains are
thoroughly coated in the oil. Pour in the wine and
cook until the grains have absorbed all the liquid.

Add a small ladleful of chicken stock to the pan,
let the rice grains absorb the liquid, then add
another ladleful of stock. Gradually add the rest
of the hot stock in this manner, always waiting
until one ladleful of stock has been completely
absorbed before adding the next.

Remove the pan from the heat and add the
butter, piece by piece, along with the grated
Parmesan, letting it rest a moment before stirring.
The risotto should take on a creamy consistency.

Serve immediately.

Saffron risotto with porcini

Serves 4
Preparation: 5 minutes
Cooking: 25 minutes

1 litre/1¾ pints/4 cups chicken stock
4 saffron threads
300 g/10 oz fresh porcini mushrooms (ceps)
2 tablespoons butter
1 onion, chopped
4 tablespoons chopped parsley
200 g/7 oz/1 cup superfine Arborio or superfine
Carnaroli rice, washed and drained
3½ tablespoons dry white wine
40 g/1½ oz/⅓ cup freshly grated Parmesan
cheese
olive oil, for cooking
salt and freshly ground black pepper

Gently heat the chicken stock in a pan. Add the saffron threads, cover, and leave to steep.

Clean the porcini; cut off their stems and coarsely dice the caps.

Melt a knob of the butter in a pan, add the chopped onion and fry until golden. Add the mushrooms, Sauté over high heat, then stir in the chopped parsley. Remove from the heat and keep warm.

Melt the remaining butter in a heavy-bottomed pan. Add the rice and sauté for a minute or so, stirring with a wooden spoon until the grains are thoroughly coated in butter. Pour in the wine and let the grains absorb all the liquid.

Remove the saffron threads from the chicken stock. Add a small ladleful of chicken stock to the pan, let the rice grains absorb the liquid, then add another ladleful of stock. Gradually add the rest of the stock in this manner, always waiting until one ladleful of stock has been completely absorbed before adding the next.

Remove the pan from the heat and add the grated Parmesan. Let the risotto rest a moment before stirring. The rice should take on a creamy consistency. Add the diced porcini and stir well.

Serve immediately.

Risotto with langoustines (Dublin Bay prawns)

Serves 4
Preparation: 5 minutes
Cooking: 25 minutes

1 litre/1¾ pints/4 cups vegetable stock
100 g/3½ oz/1 stick butter
1 onion, chopped
200 g/7 oz/1 cup superfine Arborio or superfine
Carnaroli rice, washed and drained
3½ tablespoons dry white wine
40 g/1½ oz/⅓ cup freshly grated Parmesan
cheese
20 or so langoustines (Dublin Bay prawns)
1 pinch cayenne pepper
1 garlic clove, chopped
salt and freshly ground black pepper

Gently heat the vegetable stock in a pan.

Melt 1½ tablespoons of the butter in a heavy-bottomed pan. Add the chopped onion and sweat for 2 minutes. Pour in the rice and sauté for a minute or so, stirring with a wooden spoon until the grains are thoroughly coated in butter. Pour in the wine and cook until the grains have absorbed all the liquid.

Add a small ladleful of vegetable stock to the pan, let the rice grains absorb the liquid, then add another ladleful of stock. Gradually add the rest of the stock in this manner, always waiting until one ladleful of stock has been completely absorbed before adding the next.

Remove the pan from the heat and add 1½ tablespoons of the butter and the grated Parmesan. Let the risotto rest a moment before stirring, then set aside and keep warm.

Rinse and drain the langoustines. Heat the remaining butter in a frying pan. Add the pinch of cayenne pepper and place the langoustines in the foaming butter. Turn them with a spatula, add the chopped garlic clove and cook for 4 to 5 minutes. Season with salt and pepper.

Serve the pan-fried langoustines at once accompanied by the risotto.

Risotto nero

Serves 4
Preparation: 5 minutes
Cooking: 1 hour

1 litre/1¾ pints/4 cups chicken stock
200 g/7 oz/1 cup Venere Nero wholegrain
black rice, washed and drained
1½ tablespoons butter, diced
40 g/1½ oz/⅓ cup freshly grated Parmesan
cheese
olive oil, for cooking
salt and freshly ground black pepper

Pour the chicken stock into a pan and heat gently.

Heat 2 tablespoons olive oil in a heavy-bottomed
pan. Pour in the rice, sauté for a minute or so
and stir with a wooden spoon until the grains are
thoroughly coated in oil.

Add a small ladleful of chicken stock to the pan,
let the grains of rice absorb the liquid, then add
another ladleful of stock. Gradually add the rest
of the stock in this manner, always waiting until
one ladleful of stock has been completely
absorbed before adding the next.

Remove the pan from the heat; add the diced
butter and grated Parmesan. Let the risotto rest a
moment before stirring. The rice should take on
a creamy consistency.

Serve hot.

Minestrone with mint

Serves 4
Preparation: 10 minutes
Cooking: 30 minutes

150 g/5 oz extrafine French (green) beans
1/2 red bell pepper, diced
1 celery stalk, washed and finely sliced
2 carrots, peeled and sliced into thin rounds
100 g/31/2 oz/scant 1/2 cup Arborio rice, washed and drained
100 g/31/2 oz/3/4 cup fresh or frozen peas
2 tablespoons chopped fresh mint leaves
75 g/3 oz/3/4 cup Parmesan cheese shavings
olive oil, for cooking
salt and freshly ground black pepper

Top and tail the beans; rinse, and cut into pieces about 5 cm/2 inches long.

Heat 1 tablespoon oil in a lidded casserole; add the beans, pepper, celery and carrots and sweat for a few minutes, stirring. Season with salt and pepper. Pour in 1 litre/13/4 pints/4 cups water, bring to a boil and add the rice and peas. Cover with a close-fitting lid and simmer for about 25 minutes.

Add the chopped mint leaves 5 minutes before the end of the cooking time. Season with pepper and sprinkle with the Parmesan cheese shavings just before serving.

Lentil soup with fresh coriander (cilantro)

Serves 4
Preparation: 10 minutes
Cooking: 20 minutes

600 ml/1 pint/21/2 cups chicken stock
2 onions, peeled and chopped
125 g/4 oz/1/2 cup long-grain basmati rice, washed and drained
100 g/31/2 oz/1/2 cup red lentils, rinsed
2 teaspoons cumin seeds
1 clove
1 small cinnamon stick
2 tablespoons coriander (cilantro) leaves
oil, for cooking
salt and freshly ground black pepper

Pour the chicken stock into a pan and bring to a simmer.

Heat 1 tablespoon oil in a lidded casserole and sauté the onions until golden. Lift out half the onions with a slotted spoon and reserve. Add the rice and lentils and stir round the pan. Pour in the chicken stock and add the cumin seeds, clove and cinnamon stick. Cover and cook over low heat for about 25 minutes or until the rice and lentils are cooked.

Remove the clove and cinnamon stick and leave the soup to rest for a while until you are ready to serve.

Reheat the soup and sprinkle with the reserved fried onions and coriander leaves just before serving.

Gazpacho

Serves 4
Preparation: 20 minutes
Chilling: 2 hours minimum

40 g/13/4 oz/4 tablespoons semi-brown rice, already cooked and set aside to cool
500 g/1 lb well ripened tomatoes
1 small cucumber
3 garlic cloves
5 tablespoons olive oil
1 yellow bell pepper, diced
1 onion, finely chopped
3 tablespoons aged wine vinegar
dash of Tabasco
salt and freshly ground black pepper

Place the tomatoes in a heatproof bowl and cover them with boiling water. Leave for a minute, pierce with a sharp knife, and peel the skins. Remove the seeds and dice the flesh.

Rinse and peel the cucumber and cut the flesh into small dice.

Peel and halve the garlic cloves; remove the green shoot and crush the cloves in a mortar with a small pinch of salt. Pour in the olive oil, stirring all the while, then let rest for 20 minutes.

Put the tomatoes, pepper, cucumber and onion into the goblet of a blender, add the vinegar, oil and garlic mixture, then blend everything to a smooth purée.

Add the cooked rice, season with salt and pepper and chill in the refrigerator for at least 2 hours.

Serve ice-cold with a dash of Tabasco.

Stuffed courgettes (zucchini)

Serves 4 to 6
Preparation: 25 minutes
Cooking: 55 minutes

60 g/2½ oz/6 tablespoons long-grain rice,
already cooked and set aside
1 onion, peeled and chopped
1 thyme sprig
8 to 10 small round courgettes (zucchini)
60 g/2½ oz boiled ham, chopped
1 garlic clove, finely chopped
75 g/3 oz/¾ cup freshly grated Parmesan cheese
7 basil leaves, torn into small pieces
2 eggs, beaten
olive oil, for cooking
salt and freshly ground black pepper

Preheat the oven to 180°C (350°F), gas mark 4.

Heat 1 tablespoon olive oil in a frying pan. Add
the onion and thyme sprig, and sauté gently for
5 minutes. Cook the courgettes in a large pan of
boiling water for 5 minutes. Drain, slice in half
from top to bottom and scoop out the flesh with
a small spoon.

Crush the courgette flesh with a fork, and mix it
with the sautéed onion, ham, garlic, rice,
Parmesan, chopped basil and eggs. Season with
salt and pepper.

Fill the courgette halves with the stuffing and
arrange in a gratin dish. Add about 2 tablespoons
water in the base to prevent sticking, and bake
for 25 minutes.

Stuffed aubergines (eggplant)

Serves 4
Preparation: 30 minutes
Cooking: 40 minutes

75 g/3 oz/½ cup long-grain rice, already cooked
and set aside
4 aubergines (eggplants)
300 g/10 oz/1¼ cups minced (ground) lamb
2 pinches of cinnamon
1 onion, peeled and chopped
2 tablespoons pine nuts
2 tablespoons chopped mint
2 tablespoons chopped parsley
olive oil, for cooking
salt and freshly ground black pepper

Preheat the oven to 180°C (350°F), gas mark 4.

Rinse and dry the aubergines, halve them from
top to bottom and partially hollow them out with
a small spoon. Bake for 10 minutes or so.

Heat 1 tablespoon olive oil in a pan. Season the
lamb with cinnamon, salt and pepper to taste.
Sauté the chopped onion until golden, add the
meat, rice, pine nuts, chopped mint and parsley,
then stir again.

Fill the aubergine halves with the stuffing mixture
and add about 2 tablespoons water in the base of
the baking dish to prevent them from sticking.
Return them to the oven and cook for about
another 15 minutes.

Serve hot or cold.

Stuffed tomatoes

Serves 4 to 6
Preparation: 25 minutes
Cooking: 45 minutes

60g/2½ oz/6 tablespoons long-grain rice,
already cooked and set aside
6 tomatoes
200 g/7 oz button mushrooms, sliced
3 tablespoons chopped parsley
2 eggs, beaten
40 g/1½ oz/⅓ cup freshly grated Comté cheese
1 garlic clove, finely chopped
2 tablespoons chopped basil
olive oil, for cooking
salt and freshly ground black pepper

Preheat the oven to 180°C/350°F/gas mark 4.

Wash and dry the tomatoes; slice off the tops to
make a lid and scoop out the flesh with a small
spoon, discarding the seeds.

Heat a tablespoon of olive oil in a frying pan over
medium heat and brown the mushrooms. Season
with salt and pepper, stir in the chopped parsley,
and remove from the heat.

Mix the mushrooms with the rice, eggs, cheese,
garlic and basil. Season with salt and pepper. Fill
the tomatoes with the stuffing and place in a
gratin dish with about 2 tablespoons water in
the base. Bake for about 30 minutes.

Stuffed bell peppers

Serves 4 to 6
Preparation: 20 minutes
Cooking: 45 minutes

60g/2½ oz/6 tablespoons long-grain rice,
washed and drained
4 red bell peppers
1 onion
200 g/7 oz/1 scant cup minced (ground) lamb
2–3 tablespoons pine nuts
2½ tablespoons raisins
2 eggs, beaten
olive oil, for cooking
salt and freshly ground black pepper

Bring 150 ml/5 fl oz/⅔ cup water to a boil in
a large pan. Add some salt, pour in the rice in
a steady stream and stir. Cover the pan, turn
the heat down to low and cook for about
12 minutes. The rice should be cooked, but still
retain a bit of "bite" (al dente). Drain well.

While the rice is cooking, wash and dry the
peppers, cut them in half through the stalk and
remove their seeds and membranes.

Preheat the oven to 180°C (350°F), gas mark 4.

Peel and chop the onion, then sauté it in a frying
pan in 1 tablespoon olive oil. Add the lamb,
season with salt and pepper, and mix well. Cook
over medium heat until browned. Remove from
the heat and leave to cool.

Dry-fry the pine nuts in a pan until lightly toasted.

Mix together the rice, onion, lamb, pine nuts,
raisins and eggs. Fill the pepper halves with the
stuffing mixture and place them in a gratin dish.
Add about 2 tablespoons water in the base to
prevent sticking and bake for 35 minutes.

Rice gratin with a spicy yogurt topping

Serves 4 to 6
Preparation: 20 minutes
Cooking: 40 minutes

175 g/6 oz/generous ¾ cup semi-brown rice,
already cooked and set aside
625 g/1¼ lb aubergines (eggplants)
2 onions, peeled and chopped
500 g/1 lb/2 cups minced (ground) lamb
300 g/10 oz tomatoes, peeled, seeded and
coarsely chopped
3 pinches cinnamon
1 pinch paprika
3 eggs
3½ tablespoons milk
750 g/1½ lb/3 cups creamy yogurt
2 pinches chilli powder
125 g/4 oz/1 cup freshly grated Gruyère cheese
olive oil, for cooking
salt and freshly ground black pepper

Rinse and dry the aubergines, then cut into thin
strips using a vegetable peeler. Heat 4 tablespoons
olive oil in a pan and brown the aubergine strips.
Lift from the oil with a slotted spoon and leave
to drain on kitchen paper.

Heat 1 tablespoon olive oil in the pan and sauté
the onions until translucent. Add the lamb and
tomatoes, season with salt and pepper. Stir in the
cinnamon and paprika, and cook over low heat
for about 10 minutes.

Preheat the oven to 180°C (350°F), gas mark 4.

Whisk the eggs in a large bowl and add the milk,
yogurt, and chilli powder. Mix well.

Lightly oil a gratin dish. Place a layer of aubergine
on the base of the dish and cover with the rice.
Add the meat, tomato and onion mixture. Pour
over the yogurt sauce.

Bake for about 35 minutes, sprinkling the top
with the grated Gruyère cheese five minutes
before the end of the cooking time.

Serve immediately.

PAELLA AND FRIENDS

Quick paella

Serves 4 to 6
Preparation: 15 minutes
Cooking: 25 minutes

2 boned skinless chicken breasts
150 g/5 oz chorizo
1 litre/1¾ pints/4 cups chicken stock
2 cloves garlic, finely chopped
150 g/5 oz bell pepper, seeded and diced
2 tomatoes, peeled, seeded and coarsely chopped
400 g/14 oz/2 cups short-grain rice, washed
and drained
200 g/7 oz/2 cups fresh or frozen peas
2 pinches saffron strands
1 pinch paprika
olive oil, for cooking
salt and freshly ground black pepper

Cut the chicken breasts and the chorizo into small cubes.

Gently heat the stock in a large pan.

Heat 1 tablespoon olive oil in a large paella pan and sauté the garlic until golden. Add the diced bell pepper, followed by the chicken and chorizo. Season with salt and pepper and continue to fry, stirring regularly. Add the chopped tomato, then the rice, and mix well.

Add the stock and the peas, bring to a simmer, season with salt, and add the saffron and paprika. Cover and cook for about 10 minutes. Lower the heat and cook for another 10 minutes or so until the rice is tender.

Five-vegetable paella

Serves 4 to 6
Preparation: 25 minutes
Cooking: 25 minutes

2 red bell peppers
1 aubergine (eggplant)
300 g/10 oz French (green) beans
4 artichoke hearts, cooked
4 garlic cloves
1 litre/1¾ pints/4 cups chicken stock
2 tomatoes, peeled, seeded and coarsely chopped
400 g/14 oz/1¾ cups short-grain rice, washed and drained
few pinches powdered saffron
1 pinch paprika
olive oil
salt and freshly ground black pepper

Rinse and drain the peppers, aubergine and beans. Halve the peppers, remove their seeds and ribs and finely dice the flesh.

Cut the aubergine into cubes and the beans into short lengths. Coarsely dice the artichoke hearts. Peel and halve the garlic; remove the green shoot and finely chop the cloves.

Pour the stock into a large pan and heat gently.

Heat 1 tablespoon olive oil in a large paella pan. Sauté the garlic until golden, then add the peppers, aubergine and beans. Season with salt and pepper and continue to cook, stirring regularly. Add the artichoke hearts and the chopped tomatoes.

Tip in the rice and stir until the grains are almost golden. Pour in the stock, bring to a simmer, add the saffron and paprika and season with salt to taste. Cover and cook for about 10 minutes. Lower the heat and cook for an additional 10 minutes or so until the rice is tender.

Pork, chicken and prawn (shrimp) paella

Serves 4 to 6
Preparation: 25 minutes
Cooking: 25 minutes

1 litre/1¾ pints/4 cups chicken stock
1 dozen king prawns (jumbo shrimp)
2 garlic cloves, finely chopped
250 g/8 oz boned skinless chicken breast, cubed
200 g/7 oz pork loin (fillet or tenderloin), cubed
2 tomatoes, peeled, seeded and coarsely chopped
400 g/14 oz/1¾ cups short-grain rice, washed and drained
2 pinches saffron powder
1 pinch paprika
olive oil, for cooking
salt and freshly ground black pepper

Gently heat the stock in a large pan.

Rinse and pat dry the prawns. Heat 2 tablespoons olive oil in a large paella pan. Sauté the garlic until golden, then add the prawns and fry them over medium heat for 2 minutes. Remove the prawns from the pan. Add the chicken and pork, and cook, stirring constantly, until brown on all sides. Season with salt and pepper, add the chopped tomatoes and cook for 2 minutes.

Add the rice and sauté, stirring, until the grains are almost golden. Pour in the stock and bring to a simmer. Season with salt and add the saffron and paprika; cover and cook for 10 minutes. Lower the heat, add the prawns and cook for another 10 minutes or so until the rice is tender.

Spicy Mexican rice

Serves 4
Preparation: 10 minutes
Cooking: 15 minutes

200 g/7 oz/1 cup long-grain rice, already cooked and set aside
2 courgettes (zucchini)
1 red bell pepper
chilli powder
4 tablespoons pine nuts
4 tablespoons coriander (cilantro) leaves
oil, for cooking
salt and freshly ground black pepper

Wash, top and tail the courgettes. Wash and halve the bell pepper and remove the membranes. Finely dice both vegetables.

Heat a small amount of oil in a pan. Sauté the diced vegetables for a few minutes over medium to high heat, stirring constantly. Season with salt and pepper.

Add the rice to the pan along with 2 or 3 pinches of chilli powder and stir well. Heat through for 1 or 2 minutes, then add the pine nuts.

Sprinkle with the coriander leaves and serve hot.

Rice with olives and peppers

Serves 4 to 6
Preparation: 15 minutes
Cooking: 15 minutes

1 yellow bell pepper, diced
1 red bell pepper, diced
4 tomatoes, peeled, seeded and chopped
4 garlic cloves, finely chopped
chilli powder
150 g/5 oz/1 cup pitted olives
2 onions, peeled and chopped
200 g/7 oz/1 cup long-grain rice, washed
and drained
350 ml/12 fl oz/1½ cups vegetable stock
olive oil, for cooking
salt and freshly ground black pepper

Heat 2 tablespoons olive oil in a lidded casserole. Add the diced peppers and sweat them over low heat. Add the tomatoes and the chopped garlic. Season with salt and pepper and sprinkle with a pinch of chilli powder. Cover and cook gently for 15 minutes or so, adding the olives towards the end of cooking.

While the vegetables are cooking, heat 1 table-spoon olive oil in a pan, add the chopped onions and cook until golden, stirring regularly.

Add the rice to the pan. Pour in the warm vegetable stock and bring to a simmer. Add a pinch of chilli powder, season with salt and pepper, cover, and simmer for about 15 minutes or until the rice is cooked.

Serve hot, accompanied by the vegetables.

Spicy yogurt chicken with rice

Serves 4 to 6
Preparation: 15 minutes
Cooking: 35 minutes

1 onion, cut into large chunks
2 garlic cloves, chopped
5 tablespoons chopped mint leaves + a few whole leaves for garnish
1 teaspoon grated ginger
1 teaspoon turmeric
1 teaspoon curry powder
150 g/5 oz/²/3 cup plain yogurt
2 tomatoes, peeled, seeded and coarsely chopped
1 chicken, cut into pieces
175 g/6 oz/³/4 cup long-grain basmati rice, washed and drained
oil, for cooking
salt and freshly ground black pepper

Place the onion, garlic, mint and ginger in a blender and blend until you have a smooth purée.

Heat 1 tablespoon oil in a lidded casserole. Pour in the garlic, onion, mint and ginger mixture and fry for 1 minute. Then add the turmeric and curry powder, followed by the yogurt and tomatoes, and stir to mix.

Place the chicken pieces in the pot. Stir until they are well covered with the spicy paste, then cover and cook over gentle heat for 15 to 20 minutes, adding a little water to stop them from sticking.

Heat 1 tablespoon oil in a heavy-bottomed pan. Add the rice and stir until the grains are well coated in oil. Add 300 ml/10 fl oz/1¼ cups hot water and season with salt and pepper. Bring to a simmer, lower the heat and cook gently with the lid on for about 15 minutes, or until the rice is tender.

Tip the rice onto a serving plate, top with the chicken pieces and scatter over the whole mint leaves just before serving.

Rice with prunes, dates and almonds

Serves 4 to 6
Preparation: 10 minutes
Cooking: 15 minutes

75 g/3 oz/¹/2 cup pitted prunes
75 g/3 oz/¹/2 cup raisins
2 onions, peeled and chopped
200 g/7 oz/1 cup long-grain rice, washed and drained
4–6 pitted dates
2 tablespoons blanched whole almonds
pinch of saffron
oil, for cooking
salt and freshly ground black pepper

Place the prunes and raisins in a bowl and cover with warm water.

Heat 1 tablespoon oil in a pan and sauté the onions for a minute or two, stirring regularly. Add the rice and stir to mix. Pour over 350 ml/12 fl oz/ 1¹/2 cups warm water in which the pinch of saffron has been dissolved. Season with salt and pepper, cover, and cook over low heat for about 12 to 15 minutes or until the rice is almost cooked.

5 minutes before the end of the cooking time, drain the prunes and raisins and add to the rice, along with the dates and almonds. Serve warm.

Prawn (shrimp) jambalaya

Serves 4
Preparation: 15 minutes
Cooking: 25 minutes

175 g/6 oz/³/4 cup long-grain rice, washed and drained
1 red bell pepper, halved, seeded and diced
2 onions, chopped
2 garlic cloves, finely chopped
1 stick celery, rinsed and chopped
pinch thyme
30 or so peeled prawns (shrimp)
Tabasco
knob of butter
oil, for cooking
salt and freshly ground black pepper

Cook the rice in the Creole style for 20 minutes (see method page 10). Drain and leave to cool.

Heat 1 tablespoon oil in a pan. Add the diced pepper, onions, garlic and celery. Sprinkle with the thyme. Cook for 15 minutes, stirring regularly and season with salt and pepper.

Add the prawns and a dash of Tabasco and cook for 5 minutes. Tip in the rice, stirring with a fork to stop the grains from sticking.

Add the knob of butter just before serving.

SWEET TREATS

Coconut and cardamom rice

Serves 4
Preparation: 5 minutes
Cooking: 30 minutes

500 ml/17 fl oz/2 cups milk
seeds from 2 cardamom pods, crushed to
a powder
100 g/3½ oz/½ cup short-grain pudding rice,
rinsed and drained
40 g/1½ oz/½ cup shredded coconut
3½ tablespoons brown sugar
vanilla extract, to taste

Pour the milk into a heavy-bottomed pan and
add the crushed cardamom. Bring to the boil,
then add the rice in a steady stream. Cover,
turn down the heat and cook gently for about
25 minutes.

While the rice is cooking, place the shredded
coconut into a small bowl and pour over
2 tablespoons warm water. Leave to soak for a
few minutes.

Add the brown sugar, a few drops of vanilla
extract to taste, and the rehydrated coconut to
the rice and cook gently for a further 5 minutes.

Spoon the coconut rice into individual serving
bowls and leave to cool.

Serve warm, or well chilled.

Sticky rice with banana

Serves 4 to 6
Preparation: 10 minutes
Cooking: 15 minutes
Soaking: 3 hours

100 g/3½ oz/½ cup sticky rice
3 bananas
500 ml/17 fl oz/2 cups coconut milk
5 tablespoons caster (superfine) sugar
½ teaspoon vanilla extract, or to taste

Rinse the rice, tip it into a large bowl filled with water, and leave to soak for at least 3 hours.

Rinse the rice several times more, then drain. Tip the rice into a pan, add water to cover and bring to the boil. Cook at a gentle boil for about 12 minutes.

Peel the bananas and slice them into rounds.

Place the coconut milk, sugar and vanilla extract into a second pan. Cook over low heat for 5 minutes, then add the banana. Continue cooking for another 10 minutes or so.

Allow this mixture to cool, then serve with the hot rice.

Rice pudding, pure and simple

Serves 4
Preparation: 5 minutes
Cooking: 30 minutes

500 ml/17 fl oz/2 cups milk
100 g/3½ oz/½ cup round-grain rice, rinsed and drained
4½ tablespoons caster (superfine) sugar
vanilla extract, to taste

Pour the milk into a heavy-bottomed pan. Bring to the boil, then stir in the rice in a steady stream. Cover and cook gently for about 25 minutes.

Add the sugar and vanilla extract to taste, and stir to mix. Cover the pan and cook gently for about 5 minutes more.

Spoon the rice pudding into small bowls and leave to cool before serving.

Vanilla rice pudding

Serves 4
Preparation: 10 minutes
Cooking: 25 minutes

100 g/3½ oz/½ cup semi-brown short-grain rice or wholegrain rice, washed and drained
½ vanilla pod (bean)
500 ml/17 fl oz/2 cups milk
zest of half an untreated lemon, pared into strips with a zester
4 tablespoons brown sugar
1 tablespoon butter, diced
2 egg yolks
salt

Add the rice to a large pan of lightly salted boiling water and cook over low heat for 10 minutes, Drain well.

Split the vanilla pod from top to bottom. Place the milk and pod in a heavy-bottomed pan, bring to a simmer, and add the rice and strips of lemon zest. Cover and cook gently for about 10 minutes.

Add the brown sugar and remove the pan from the heat. Stir, while adding the butter, piece by piece. Let cool for a few minutes.

Whisk the egg yolks in a bowl and add to the rice pudding. Cook gently for 5 minutes more, stirring regularly.

Remove the vanilla pod and lemon zest, spoon the rice into small bowls and leave to cool.

Caramel rice pudding

Serves 4
Preparation: 5 minutes
Cooking: 30 minutes

500 ml/17 fl oz/2 cups milk
100 g/3½ oz/½ cup short-grain pudding rice, washed and drained
2½ tablespoons caster (superfine) sugar
vanilla extract, to taste
bottled caramel sauce

Pour the milk into a heavy-bottomed pan. Bring to a boil, then stir in the rice in a slow, steady stream. Cover and cook over low heat for about 25 minutes.

Add the sugar and vanilla extract to taste, and stir to mix. Cover, and cook for about 5 minutes more.

Transfer the rice pudding to small bowls and leave in a cool place until ready to serve.

Just before serving, pour a little caramel sauce over each bowl.

Chocolate rice pudding

Serves 4
Preparation: 5 minutes
Cooking: 30 minutes

5 tablespoons unsweetened cocoa powder
500 ml/17 fl oz/2 cups milk
1 small cinnamon stick
100 g/3½ oz/½ cup short-grain pudding rice, washed and drained
4 tablespoons brown sugar

Mix the cocoa powder with 3 or 4 tablespoons of the milk.

Place the remaining milk, dissolved cocoa powder, and the cinnamon stick in a heavy-bottomed pan. Bring to a boil, then add the rice in a slow, steady stream. Cover and cook over low heat for about 25 minutes.

Add the brown sugar, stir to mix, cover, and cook for another 5 minutes.

Pour the chocolate rice pudding into small bowls and leave to cool.

Rice pudding with maple syrup

Serves 4
Preparation: 5 minutes
Cooking: 25 minutes

500 ml/17 fl oz/2 cups milk
100 g/3½ oz/½ cup short-grain pudding rice,
washed and drained
4 tablespoons maple syrup

Pour the milk into a heavy-bottomed pan. Bring
to a boil, then add the rice in a slow, steady
stream. Cover and cook over low heat for about
20 minutes.

Add the maple syrup, cover and cook for about
5 minutes longer.

Pour the rice pudding into small bowls and leave
to cool.

Rice pudding with chocolate-coated caramel bars

Serves 4
Preparation: 5 minutes
Cooking: 30 minutes

500 ml/17 fl oz/2 cups milk
2 chocolate-coated caramel bars
100 g/3½ oz/½ cup short-grain pudding rice,
washed and drained
2 tablespoons caster (superfine) sugar

Place the milk and the caramel bars in a heavy-
bottomed pan. Bring to the boil, turn down the
heat to low and let the caramel bars melt.

Stir well, then add the rice in a slow, steady
stream. Cover and cook over low heat for about
25 minutes.

Stir in the sugar, cover, and cook for another
5 minutes.

Pour the rice pudding into small bowls and leave
to cool.

Rice pudding with candied orange peel

Serves 4
Preparation: 5 minutes
Cooking: 30 minutes

500 ml/17 fl oz/2 cups milk
100 g/3½ oz/½ cup short-grain pudding rice,
washed and drained
grated rind of an untreated orange
40 g/1½ oz candied orange peel, diced
3 tablespoons caster (superfine) sugar
1 pinch salt

Pour the milk into a heavy-bottomed pan. Bring
to the boil, add the pinch of salt, the rice and
the grated orange rind. Cover and cook over low
heat for about 25 minutes.

Stir in the diced candied orange peel and the
sugar. Cover and cook for about 5 minutes more.

Pour the rice pudding into small bowls and leave
to cool.

Rice with mango

Serves 4 to 6
Preparation: 5 minutes
Cooking: 10 minutes
Soaking: 1 hour

200 g/7 oz/1 cup sticky rice
2 tablespoons brown sugar
250 ml/8 fl oz/1 cup coconut milk
4 tablespoons warm water
1 ripe mango

Place the rice in a large bowl and add water to cover. Soak for at least 1 hour. Rinse and drain the rice, then tip it into the centre of a dish towel.

Heat some water in a steamer. Place the dish towel containing the rice in the basket, taking care to spread out the rice in an even layer. Fold over the edges. Cover and cook for about 10 minutes.

Open up the cloth, let cool for a minute, then tip the rice onto a deep plate, heaping it up nicely.

Place the brown sugar, coconut milk and warm water in a pan; stir and bring to a simmer. Remove the pan from the heat.

Pour the coconut-milk syrup over the rice and leave to cool.

Transfer to a serving dish and, just before serving, add the mango, cut into slices.

Rice with saffron and peaches in syrup

This recipe takes rather longer to prepare, though it is very easy – a simple and sophisticated dessert.

Serves 4
Preparation: 25 minutes
Cooking: 30 minutes
Soaking: 30 minutes
Chilling: 2 hours

100 g/3½ oz/½ cup long-grain basmati rice, washed and drained
500 ml/17 fl oz/2 cups milk
pinch saffron threads
pinch of salt
2 tablespoons flaked (slivered) almonds
3 tablespoons clear honey
4 ripe peaches
1 tablespoon butter
oil, for cooking

Put the rice into a bowl and add water to cover. Leave to soak for 30 minutes, then drain carefully.

Gently heat the milk in a heavy-bottomed pan; add the saffron strands and a pinch of salt, cover, and leave to infuse for 10 minutes.

Heat a small amount of oil in a pan or flameproof casserole; tip in the rice and sauté for a minute or two. Add the almonds.

Remove the saffron strands from the milk, add 2 tablespoons of the honey to the hot milk, stir and pour over the rice and almonds. Cover and cook over low heat for about 20 minutes.

In the meantime, bring a large pan of water to a simmer. Blanch the peaches for 1 minute, then refresh them under cold running water. Skin and quarter the peaches.

Heat the remaining tablespoon of honey with the butter in a pan. Add the peach quarters and cook them gently for about 2 minutes, then turn and cook for an additional 3 minutes.　:

Fluff up the rice with a fork, and firmly pack it into ramekins, cups, or glasses. Leave to chill in the refrigerator for at least 2 hours.

When ready to serve, turn the rice out onto individual plates, spoon the peach quarters at the side and scatter with the almonds.

Coconut rice with peaches

Serves 4
Preparation: 5 minutes
Cooking: 30 minutes
Chilling: 1 hour

500 ml17 fl oz/2 cups milk
100 g/3½ oz/½ cup short-grain pudding rice, rinsed and drained
40 g/1½ oz/½ cup unsweetened shredded coconut
4½ tablespoons caster (superfine) sugar
vanilla extract, to taste
4 ripe peaches
dash lemon juice

Pour the milk into a heavy-bottomed pan. Bring to the boil, then add the rice in a steady stream. Cover and cook over low heat for about 25 minutes.

Add the shredded coconut, sugar, and vanilla extract to taste. Stir, cover and cook gently for another 5 minutes. Pour the coconut rice into small bowls and chill in the refrigerator for at least an hour.

Blanch the peaches as in the recipe on the left, then peel and quarter them and reduce to a smooth purée in a blender. Sprinkle with a dash of lemon juice.

Serve the rice well chilled with the peach purée.

Spiced rice pudding with coconut

Serves 4
Preparation: 15 minutes
Cooking: 30 minutes
Soaking: 30 minutes

100 g/3½ oz/½ cup long-grain basmati rice, washed and drained
500 ml/17 fl oz/2 cups milk
1 clove
1 small cinnamon stick
4½ tablespoons caster (superfine) sugar
vanilla extract, to taste
50 g/2 oz/⅔ cup unsweetened shredded coconut

Put the rice into a large bowl and add water to cover. Soak for 30 minutes, then drain carefully.

Heat the milk, clove, cinnamon stick, sugar, and vanilla extract to taste in a heavy-bottomed pan. Bring to a simmer, then add the rice, stir, cover and cook over low heat for 25 minutes.

Dry-fry the shredded coconut in a pan, stirring constantly, until nicely toasted.

Remove the clove and cinnamon stick from the pan. Pour the rice into small bowls. Leave to cool, then sprinkle with the toasted coconut.

Cream of rice with orange-flower water

If you are able to track down the delicious instant Crème de Riz, so loved by the French, this is a simple, easy dessert that makes an excellent companion for a fruit compote or dried fruit soaked in brandy or a favourite liqueur.

Serves 4
Preparation: 5 minutes
Cooking: 10–12 minutes

6 tablespoons cream of rice (Crème de Riz)
1 litre/1¾ pints/4 cups milk
100 g/3½ oz/½ cup caster (superfine) sugar
2 tablespoons orange-flower water
60 g/2½ oz/½ cup pistachios (shelled weight), chopped

Mix the cream of rice with 3 tablespoons milk. Pour the remaining milk and the dissolved cream of rice into a heavy-bottomed pan; stir to mix and bring to a simmer. Cover and cook over low heat for about 10 minutes, stirring regularly.

Add the sugar and the orange-flower water; stir, and remove pan from heat.

Pour the cream of rice into small bowls and leave to cool. Sprinkle with chopped pistachios and serve at room temperature.

Note: Cooking time will vary depending on the type of cream of rice used (instant or otherwise).

Rice pudding with pan-fried apples

This rice pudding may be prepared in advance, though the apples should be pan-fried at the last minute. If you are fond of calvados you may wish to flambé the apples in the liqueur at the end of cooking.

Serves 4
Preparation: 5 minutes
Cooking: 30 minutes

500 ml/17 fl oz/2 cups milk
100 g/3½ oz/½ cup short-grain pudding rice, rinsed and drained
6 tablespoons caster (superfine) sugar
vanilla extract, to taste
4 apples (Cox's Orange Pippins, Braeburns, Jonagolds...)
1 tablespoon honey
1 tablespoon butter

Pour the milk into a heavy-bottomed pan. Bring to the boil, then add the rice in a steady stream. Cover, reduce heat and cook gently for about 25 minutes.

Add 3 tablespoons of the sugar and vanilla extract to taste. Stir, cover and cook for about 5 minutes. Pour the rice pudding into small bowls and leave to cool.

Peel and core the apples and slice them into large wedges. Melt the honey, the remaining sugar and the butter in a pan. Add the apples and pan-fry until they pick up a bit of colour. Cook for a few minutes more, then serve with the rice pudding.

APPENDICES

List of recipes

Index of recipes

Shopping and table settings:
Pauline Ricard-André

Cutlery
Le Bon Marché Rive Gauche: p. 37
WMF: pp. 60, 133, 149

Plates, platters and pans
Asa: p. 42
Habitat: pp. 47, 83

Bowls, cups and glassware
Facteur Céleste: pp. 61, 71, 123, 124
Home Autour du Monde: p. 60
Ceramica Blue: pp. 27, 32, 33, 89, 111, 147, 148
The Conran Shop: p. 90
Habitat: pp. 35, 63, 139
Greenage: pp. 29, 38, 93 (platter), 151
Le Bon Marché Rive Gauche: pp. 57, 109
Lafayette Maison: p. 50

Tablecloths, fabrics, placemats and accessories
Le Bon Marché Rive Gauche: pp. 35, 45, 59, 63, 70, 90, 99, 101
Facteur Céleste: pp. 38, 39, 40, 42, 50, 51, 61, 123
Robert le Héros: p. 57

Addresses

ASA
department stores or sales outlets
tel: 00 49 26 24 189 45.

LE BON MARCHÉ RIVE GAUCHE
24 rue de Sèvres, 75007 Paris.

FACTEUR CÉLESTE
38 rue Quincampoix, 75004 Paris.

WMF
department stores
tel: 01 44 74 18 81.

GREENAGE
98 rue du Bac, 75007 Paris.

HOME AUTOUR DU MONDE
8 rue des Francs Bourgeois, 75004 Paris.

CERAMICA BLUE
10 Bleinheim Crescent, Notting Hill
London W11 1NN
www.ceramicablue.co.uk

ROBERT LE HÉROS
13 rue de Saintonge, 75003 Paris.

LAFAYETTE MAISON
35 bd Haussmann 75009 Paris.

Thanks to:
Marie and Nathaly for their kitchens, and Ambroise and Junko for their enthusiastic participation in the camerawork.

Cadbury France for permission to reproduce the Carambars on page 143, and their use in the superb 'Rice pudding with chocolate-coated caramel bars' recipe.

This edition © Marabout (Hachette Livre) 2004
This edition published by Hachette Illustrated UK, Octopus Publishing Group,
2–4 Heron Quays, London E14 4JP

English translation by JMS Books LLP (email: moseleystrachan@dsl.pipex.com)
Translation © Octopus Publishing Group

A CIP catalogue for this book is available from the British Library

ISBN 10: 1 84430 162 1

ISBN 13: 978 1 84430 162 1

Printed by Toppan Printing Co., (HK) Ltd.